PEOPLE OVER CAPITAL:

The Co-operative Alternative to Capitalism

Acknowledgements

First, we should thank all the authors submitting entries to the 2012 Prize – not just those that are reproduced here. Entrants came from all walks of life and submissions arrived from as far afield as Argentina and Italy. Giles Simon and the communications team at Co-operatives UK played an important role in getting news of the competition out into the wider world.

Essays with the authors' names removed were distributed to the four judges, whom we also thank:

- Ed Mayo – Secretary General, Co-operatives UK
- Rob Harrison – Director, Ethical Consumer
- Paul Fitzgerald – Radical Political Cartoonist (with help from Eva Schlunke)
- Katy Brown – Director, Ethical Consumer

Thanks to Liz Chater and Jane Tuner at Ethical Consumer for administrative support for the submissions and judging process. Adele Armistead provided the web design and Tom Chafer-Cook the web programming for the Co-operative Alternatives website which helped to promote the project. Thanks also to Demetrio Guzzardi for working on the references. Thanks to Dan Raymond-Barker (marketing) and Chris Brazier (editing) at New Internationalist for their invaluable help with bringing this book to light.

And, last but not least, thanks to Unicorn Grocery, Co-operatives UK and *Ethical Consumer* magazine readers for their financial support for the project.

PEOPLE OVER CAPITAL:

The Co-operative Alternative to Capitalism

Edited by
Rob Harrison

Foreword by
Ed Mayo
(Co-operatives UK)

New Internationalist ethical consumer

People Over Capital: The Co-operative Alternative to Capitalism
First published in 2013 by
New Internationalist Publications Ltd
55 Rectory Road
Oxford OX4 1BW, UK
newint.org

Front cover design: Andrew Kokotka/New Internationalist.

Printed by TJ International Ltd, Cornwall, UK
who hold environmental accreditation ISO 14001.

British Library Cataloguing-in-Publication Data
A catalogue record for this book is available from the British Library.

Library of Congress Cataloging-in-Publication Data
A catalog record for this book is available from the Library of Congress.

ISBN 978-1-78026-161-4

Contents

Foreword

Ed Mayo

If the claim of capitalism is that a system focused on and oriented around the accumulation of capital best serves society overall, then the idea of co-operation is its natural opposite. Co-operative models of economic life are focused on forms of wealth creation in which the needs of capital are subservient to the interests of people involved. It is a simple enough contrast, generating a wealth of insight included within the contributions of this book, and it does reflect an enduring challenge – in economic life, is money our servant or our master?

Co-operative enterprises are member-owned businesses with some distinctive characteristics in terms of form and ethos. At an abstract level, the nature of co-operatives is defined by a co-operative identity statement proclaimed by the International Co-operative Alliance in 1995. These were endorsed by United Nations Guidelines in 2001, by an International Labour Organization Recommendation (193) in 2002, and have now been written into many co-operative laws around the world.

In practice, there is a diversity of co-operative forms in the UK and overseas. Apart from the investors of capital, there are three main economic stakeholders in any business: its consumers, the producers who supply inputs to or take the outputs from the business, and its employees. In a co-operative, usually one of these other stakeholders is put at the centre of the business as member owners. There are, therefore, four groups of co-operatives: consumer owned, producer owned, employee owned and multi-stakeholder combinations or hybrids of these. There is also continuous experimentation around key issues, such as the nature of membership, interest in community benefit and new models of financing.

The co-operative business model has a strong presence across a range of international markets. There are more than 800 million members of co-operatives in the world. Between them, they employ over 100 million people. This is 20 per cent more than the multinational enterprises. The largest 300 co-operatives in the world have an annual turnover of $1.1 trillion. In a few countries, co-operatives may have a dominant role in the economy.

The market share of co-operative enterprises provides a practical demonstration of the value that can be created on the basis of co-operative principles. In Finland, the co-operative sector is said to account for 21 per cent of GDP, in Switzerland 16 per cent and in Sweden 13 per cent. In Switzerland, for example, two societies dominate retail trade: Co-op Suisse and Migros, the latter having originally been a private company that was donated by its owner to its customers. They have a market share of 17 per cent and 32 per cent respectively. In New Zealand the largest domestic business, Fonterra, is a co-operative. Meanwhile, three-quarters of all fair trade goods are produced by co-operatives in developing countries.

Today, new technologies are reducing the barriers to mass participation and allowing an ever-widening circle of people to engage online in collaborative communities. In Charles Leadbeater's words, we are passing from an economy of 'by', 'from' and 'to', to an economy of 'with'. 'In the 20th century', he writes, 'we were identified by what we owned; in the 21st century we will also be defined by how we share and what we give away.'

As discussed in some of the essays in this book, Wikipedia is a collaborative encyclopaedia project beyond the dreams of Robert Owen. Open source software is similarly based on collaborative volunteering and now accounts for 80 per cent of the software on computer servers worldwide. In health, for almost every chronic disease there are mutual support websites and email lists, many of them global. In the arts, creative collectives are emerging as new forms of mutual aid. In education, mutual learning sites have multiplied and there has been a proliferation of web-based communities of practice.

Robin Murray, who has contributed the first chapter in this book, produced a review of the UK co-operative sector in 2010 called *Co-operation in the Age of Google*. In it, he concludes that:

'*all these and a multitude of other examples are co-operatives without walls. Their practices reflect many of the seven co-operative principles: voluntary and open membership, member participation, autonomy and independence, education and information, and connection to other related groups. Their forms of democracy vary. What is distinct about them is that their inputs, their outputs and their distribution are largely free. People contribute voluntarily. There is open access to the outputs on the condition that any use made of them is also free. It is at heart a gift economy, based on core principles of co-operation – reciprocity and mutual respect.*'

So, does putting people at the centre of the equation make a difference? There is some evidence that engaging in co-operative enterprise helps to refresh the wellsprings of social reciprocity. There is an increasing recognition in micro-economics that institutional form can have an impact on norms and behaviour around fairness. Much of this work takes an empirical, rather than a philosophical, view as to what people think and how they behave in relation to fairness. The pioneers of this approach include the great co-operative theorists of our day – Herbert Gintis, Samuel Bowles, Ernest Fehr, Elinor Ostrom and Johnston Birchall. They are spearheading a renewal of contemporary research and thinking that is putting human behaviour and social norms of co-operation at the heart of social and economic thinking. Fairness emerges as a key factor that encourages us to be co-operative in the expectation that others will be too. Perhaps not surprisingly, 75 per cent of people associate co-operative businesses with acting fairly, compared to 18 per cent for shareholder companies. Meanwhile, people who are members of co-operatives tend statistically to be more likely than others to feel good about the state of equal opportunities across the country and more likely to feel that there is help for those in need.

The beauty of this book is that contributors have the opportunity to explore the alternatives we have to a King Midas economy that turns resources and relationships into gold, unable to value what is not financial capital. Co-operation is hard, they suggest, while never forgetting that, at least as it seems to me, true capitalism is impossible. To deal with contemporary challenges of inequality and climate change, we need co-operation at all levels. The values of co-operative self-help and mutual aid are more relevant than ever for those who wish to see shared prosperity and the emergence of a sustainable economy.

Ed Mayo
Secretary General of Co-operatives UK, www.uk.coop

Introduction
Rob Harrison

Background to this book

The global banking collapse of 2008 left pretty much every major economic institution across the Western world looking pretty stupid. Profit-seeking banks combining enormous bonuses with terrible investment decisions looked stupid. Governments, which had been persuaded that light-touch regulation of capital markets was a good idea, didn't look too clever either. And economists, whose ideological commitment to the idea of self-correcting markets blinded them to the approaching collapse, hung their heads in shame.

Quite early on after the meltdown, people began to spot that co-operative and mutual institutions had, to a large extent, come out of the crisis looking less idiotic than most.[1] And, in the years after the crisis, an increasingly confident co-operative movement began to put out statistics showing a growing co-operative sector that could be set against generally stagnant or declining economies elsewhere.

By 2011, when the real-world economic impacts of bailing out failed banks really began to bite, the idea of an Occupy movement caught the imagination of millions of people, and popular protests took place simultaneously in more then 1,000 cities around the world. The movement was very effective at expressing anger against the major economic institutions and against capitalism as an economic system, but less effective at communicating a coherent alternative strategy.

An essay prize

With some skilled good timing, the United Nations designated 2012 as the International Year of Co-operatives. In late 2011, the team at Ethical Consumer – a research and campaigning co-operative – came up with the idea of a 2012-related essay prize. If people were asked to answer the provocative question 'is there a co-operative alternative to capitalism?' then they would be encouraged to write and think about this subject at what might prove to be a particularly apposite time. Do co-operatives offer an alternative model of social organization which could address financial instability, global justice and sustainability? Or do they simply offer another way of organizing businesses within a predominantly capitalist economy? Has the modern co-operative movement become too polite and perhaps unambitious about what it could seek to achieve? Certainly in previous centuries co-operators were often writing stirring polemic about their vision of a future 'co-operative commonwealth'. From the Rochdale Pioneers in Victorian England to Canadian socialists in the inter-war years of the 20th century, the idea of a future where all businesses were co-operatively run was never far from view. Would other people share the view that co-operation might offer some kind of systemic alternative? Would the essay prize generate some great writing or powerful insights?

Arranging the chapters

This book is mainly made up of the best entries we received. Some are erudite and backed up by long lists of references. Others are more poetic. But they all contain writing of quality and passion. You can't really come away from this book – even from the more critical essays – without being encouraged by the shared desire for change and a shared vision for something much bigger.

Because each essay is designed as a stand-alone piece, there's no particular need to read the book in order. However, if you are new to co-operatives, or a bit rusty on key elements of the movement's history, then beginning with Section 1 might help. Chapters 1 and 2 are exceptions in that they were not submissions to the essay prize. They were, however, great articles asking the same question that were published in radical journals in 2012 as a reflection on the International Year of Co-operatives and bring new ideas and information to the debate.

The chapters are separated into six themed sections to help give shape to the discussion: History; Economics; Networking; Sustainability; Social Economy and Critical Perspectives. Most authors, though, range pretty widely across the subject, and some address all six areas in some depth.

Ethical Consumer and its partners in this project are UK-based, which makes this discussion somewhat inevitably UK-focused. Contributors from Canada (providing Chapters 2 and 11) and Italy (Chapter 12) do, however, help to give a somewhat wider perspective to what is, after all, a properly global movement. Cheryl Lans (Chapter 11) also observes that in 'Brazil, Spain, Argentina, Colombia and Venezuela... networks of co-operatives have proved transformative for poor people and are not mere visions of future utopian societies'.

When we judged the essays and chose the chapters for this book we did it without really knowing who the authors were. Only at the end of the process did we ask them for biographies and, unsurprisingly, none of the contributors are famous in the normal sense of the word. They are ordinary people, but ordinary people who bring decades of experience working with co-operatives, on political change or as policy advisers and academics. Their biographies are reproduced from page 228.

Unexpected insights

In any journey, it is often the things you don't expect which leave the most lasting impression. Perhaps the most attractive way for co-operatives to crowd out capitalist businesses is simply to out-compete them on their own limited terms – that is, in price and quality. We learn from Nic Wistreich, in Chapter 7, how this has, to a significant extent, been happening in the world of software and internet infrastructure. Open source software is created co-operatively and altruistically 'outside of the capitalist conception of competition and financial incentive'. It now sits behind the Android mobile operating system which powers more smartphones than the iPhone; the majority of web browsers, including Firefox, Safari and Chrome; the majority of content-management systems such as Wordpress, Drupal and Joomla; and hundreds of coding languages, including PHP, which powers Facebook and Wikipedia, Python, which powers Google and YouTube, and Ruby, which powers Twitter. Open source is a movement distinct from the formal co-operative movement but has a lot to teach us about what a more diverse and complex co-operative alternative might look like.

In Chapter 4, Dan Gregory tells us that, to answer the question 'is there a co-operative alternative to capitalism?', it might be worth looking beyond 'simply more co-operatives playing the capitalist game'. He goes on to explain how the idea of co-operation 'not only within but also between' different sectors of the economy could bring about a more efficient, 'successful, balanced and mutually supporting democratic mixed economy'.

Many of the essays identify how shareholder-focused profit-seeking corporations lie at the root of some of the systemic problems we face. Indeed, Steve Mandel, in Chapter 10, argues that replacing these kind of businesses with co-operatives will be essential for a sustainable future. Cheryl Lans in Chapter 11 reminds us, though, that co-operatives are just one alternative business model of many which address this problem. The broader social economy includes charities, non-profits, NGOs, ethical businesses, fair-trade organizations, women's groups, anti-poverty groups and some trades unions. For many people, often in countries with a culture of discourse around 'solidarity economics', co-operatives are central to their future vision of an alternative to capitalism – but so are a whole range of other social-economy organizations. As Arianna Lovera reflects in Chapter 12, the term 'solidarity economics' encompasses all organizations 'which value the notion of solidarity, as opposed to that of competitive individualism, which characterizes the dominant economic behaviour in capitalist societies'.

Environmental promise

Although addressing the structural causes of the current financial crisis is important, in many ways the most serious accusation laid at the door of modern capitalism is its apparent inability to deliver anything other than dangerously unsustainable societies. In addition, there is much evidence that profit-seeking businesses – capitalism's primary institutions – have been instrumental in obstructing effective international co-operation to address key environmental issues such as climate change. Ethical Consumer's main area of study is civil-society interventions in markets for social goals. This includes subjects such as Greenpeace boycotts of polluting companies as well as the growth of fair trade and organic labelling. We are also involved in benchmarking companies on social and environmental issues. In our research, co-operatives outperform their profit-seeking competitors on environmental responsibility most, but not all, of the time. Is there something about co-operatives that makes them inherently more environmentally conscious?

Most of the writers have addressed this question, with Chapters 9 and 10, in Section 4, focusing on this in particular. We also learn from James Doran in Chapter 6, for example, how the democratic nature of co-operatives means that the business owners may themselves be the 'externalities' that profit-seeking businesses seek to ignore. He also discusses how important it is in this context to distinguish between the profit-making aim of co-operatives and the profit-maximizing aim of capitalist firms.

However, some questions remain unanswered. Is there something in the type of co-operative which makes it more likely to follow a sustainable path? Ethical Consumer's research tends to show workers' co-operatives to be most sensitive to sustainability issues, with consumer co-operatives a close second – though not in every case. Secondary co-operatives – commonly of agricultural producers – are less likely to display sector-leading sustainability characteristics. More work remains to be done.

Co-operation as an ideology

It could be said that the idea for this book was born in the midst of a threefold crisis: a financial crisis affecting Western economies; an environmental crisis of unsustainable resource use; and a crisis of ideas whereby clear alternatives to capitalism appeared to be in short supply. Robbie Smith in Chapter 8 is one of a few contributors who specifically reflect on the idea that the current financial crisis is occurring at a time when faith in Marxism – historically the most coherent alternative to capitalism – has largely ebbed away. Other writers, particularly those in the critical perspectives section at the end, are less ready to give up on either Marxist analysis or solutions. However, the idea that co-operation could simply step in as a fully formed replacement for Marxism in public discourse, though tempting, might be ultimately unhelpful.

Daniel Crowe's contribution in Chapter 5 raises the idea that co-operatives could somehow offer more than both capitalism and Marxism. 'Co-operation is more than another economic system, a business model or a simple way of meeting social and individual needs through the pursuit of self-interest. Co-operation is a profound and revelatory concept that offers a holistic approach and practical route to achieving fundamental social, economic and political objectives.'

And then there is the issue of human fulfilment. Reflections on happiness, such as those in Chapter 6 and elsewhere, also suggest that co-operatives can help people to replace material aspirations with more human ones. Under capitalism, the focus on individualism and material wealth has been widely attributed as a cause of falling levels of happiness in advanced Western economies. If well-being is inextricably linked to our relationships with others, then co-operatives may be providing something more than just another economic system.

In Chapter 1, Robin Murray quotes Elinor Ostrom (the Nobel Prize-winning economist) writing about what is required for a sustainable future as follows: 'Extensive empirical research leads me to argue that, instead, a core goal of public policy should be to facilitate the developments of institutions that bring out the best in humans.'

Encouraging dissent

In Section 6, both chapters answer 'no' to the question 'is there a co-operative alternative to capitalism?' and give an important critical perspective. In the final chapter Chris Tomlinson provides a relatively negative view of both co-operatives and their potential as an alternative. He argues that co-operatives always have to compete with mainstream businesses on price and can therefore only afford minor social and environmental interventions without becoming uncompetitive. However much we may disagree with his analysis, or indeed with those in other chapters, a commitment to democratic participation is only serious if all views – including inconvenient ones – are heard. If co-operatives are to thrive, they need the confidence to welcome critical voices – as indeed capitalism generally does – without becoming too defensive.

John Restakis is one of the most prominent thinkers and promoters of co-operation working in this area and is referred to through this book. He explains how 'advocating the transformation of all economic institutions into co-operatives...

would be folly' and would make the co-operative model 'an instrument of yet another controlling ideology, this time one that would turn co-operation into an authoritarian dogma.'[2]

Not the end of the story?

There is no doubt that the extent to which a more co-operative future is achievable will be affected by the degree to which the co-operative movement globally wishes to, or can, articulate a collective vision. John Restakis again explains: 'This means a much more political vision for the movement, and a linking of the movement to those social and political currents that are at the forefront of the struggle for global justice.'[2]

Of course, there are practical steps to take to make such visions a reality. Many contributors make suggestions but Chapter 8 in particular bristles with ideas. In the Afterword we have reproduced the results of a public voting project to select 'one thing that would make co-operation the dominant business model'.

The top five, paraphrased, are:

1. Formal teaching about co-operatives across all educational institutions.
2. An eighth International Co-operative Principle on environmental sustainability.
3. Co-ordinated networking or 'shoaling' of co-operatives in specific industries to help them compete.
4. Communicating that co-operatives are committed to values other than profit.
5. Persuading consumers to choose co-operative products because of the movement's values.

Reading the chapters in this book certainly feels like the beginning rather than the end of the discussion. And if this project continues to be successful in attracting resources, then a second essay prize may in future lead to a second volume. In the meantime, if you want to find out which essays won the four prizes available in 2012, or if you feel like joining the discussion or commenting on what you have read, then we have web pages and a forum with more information at: ethicalconsumer.org/cooperativealternative.aspx

Perhaps next time it will be your essay that wins.

Rob Harrison

Editor of *Ethical Consumer*, ethicalconsumer.org

1 *Ethical Consumer*, May 2009, nin.tl/12QEbYy 2 John Restakis (2010) *Humanizing the Economy: Co-operatives in the age of capital*, New Society Publishers, 2010, p 248.

History and current opportunities

1
The potential for an alternative economy

Robin Murray

The first great surge of co-operation took place in Britain at
the dawn of the age of railways in the 1840s. It was a consumer
co-operation of the industrial working class. Within 50 years
it had grown into a network of more than 1,000 retail co-ops
and a wholesale society that had become the largest corporate
organization in the world. By the First World War, British co-
ops accounted for 40 per cent of food distribution. They owned
their own factories, farms, shipping lines, banks, an insurance
company and even a tea plantation in Ceylon (now Sri Lanka).
The co-operative movement was, in the vision of one of its
inspired organizers, JTW Mitchell, on the way to developing an
alternative economy.

There were similar movements of small farmers and artisans
on the continent and in North America, and later in Asia.
Common to them all was an emphasis on civic and workplace
democracy, autonomy, the quality of work and on small-scale
units gathered into large federated organizations where a larger
scale was necessary.

This way of thinking about an economy did not chime with

the model of mass production that became the dominant 20th-century paradigm for industry as well as for the principal state-centred (and centralized) alternatives on the left. The forward march of co-operation was halted.

In the past 30 years, though, there has been a rapid growth of all kinds of initiatives in the social economy. Confidence was lost in the centralized state-based alternatives, particularly after 1989. The revolution in information and communications made it possible to develop much more distributed systems of organization, with complex webs of collaboration. Now, with the financial collapse of 2008 putting neoliberalism on the back foot, we are witnessing a new interest in co-operation.

There has been a spate of books by evolutionary biologists on humanity's deep-rooted dependence on co-operation and by sociologists on the skills required for it. To general astonishment, the 2009 Nobel Prize for Economics was given to Elinor Ostrom for her work on the social economics of the commons. And co-operation runs as a common thread through the discussions of alternatives across the Occupy movement. As one of the Occupy Wall Street activists put it, they wanted a world of 'co-operatives, credit unions and fair trade'.

What should we make of all this? What part can co-operatives play in a 21st-century model of an alternative economy? Could co-operatives become the dominant form of enterprise just as joint-stock companies were in the industrial era? Can the state – itself part of the social economy – find a way of working with them in new collaborative ways? Can it indeed internalize not only co-operation's values but its practices? Can we imagine a model of the co-operative economy that generates as much confidence as once did the various versions of Fordist socialism?

The financial sector

Let's start with finance. Instead of a financial system dominated by a few centralized global banks that have subordinated production to their logic, can we imagine one with a thousand local banks, owned either by their members or municipalities? They would be a repository of local savings and lend them to small enterprises and households in need, whom they would know as intimately as the English country banks knew their neighbourhoods in the early 19th century.

For larger investments and technical support the banks would form their own regional and national bodies. And for the major strategic tasks, there would be a national public bank that would provide funds and advice to the local ones.

These were the dreams of 19th-century co-operators throughout Europe and North America. Today in Britain they would be seen as green utopianism. Yet in Germany they are part of everyday life. There are more than 1,100 independent co-operative banks, with 13,000 branches and 16 million members. In almost every neighbourhood in Germany you will find a co-operative bank, and usually on the other side of the street in co-operative competition will be one of the 15,600 branches of the 430 municipal savings banks or Sparkassen. That is more than 1,500 independent local banks with almost 30,000 branches.

Both the mutual and municipal banks have their own regional and national clearing and specialist banks. Together they dominate retail banking, with the commercial banks confined to less than a third of banking business. The public development bank, the KfW, commits more than 20 billion euros each year to finance the switch away from nuclear energy and to meet its climate-change targets. They need a highly granular banking network to reach the households and small enterprises that are key to the new energy model. That is provided by the co-operative and Sparkassen banks. These two social pillars of Germany's 'three pillar' system have been a principal factor behind the economic success of the small and medium industrial enterprises of the German 'Mittelstand'.

This model of co-operative banking was developed in the

mountainous rural areas in the 1850s to support the local farmers, small traders and artisans ignored by commercial banks, and later in the eastern cities to fund urban artisans and traders. It spread all over Germany and to much of the continent, where it still plays a major part in the national banking systems. In Holland, for example, the second-largest bank (one of the top 30 in the world) is the Rabobank, a confederation of 141 local credit unions. Like the German co-operative banks, and the similarly inspired networks in Canada, they are geared to the welfare of their local economies.

The industrial sector

What about industry? Can we imagine a co-operative region that holds its own in a globalized economy? It might equip its farmers and artisans with the most modern equipment, and help them to form co-operatives to sell their products all over the world. Each town could focus on a particular product so that it developed the necessary specialisms. It could have its own college where the skills of one generation are passed on to the next. The finance would come from local co-operative or public banks, the loans guaranteed by other artisans in the town, and all the invoices and accounting would be handled by a dense network of joint book-keepers and accountants.

This is a description of the region of Emilia Romagna in Italy. Many of the light industries there and in neighbouring regions have not just held their own but become leaders in their sector in Europe. In the ceramics town of Imola the main co-operative is now the largest ceramic producer in Europe. Carpi is one of the major clothing areas in the EU – a town of 60,000 people with 4,000 artisan firms. The Emilian farmers not only supply the local co-operative supermarkets that dominate retailing in the province but they have established their own co-operative processing and branding. Parmesan cheese is made by a co-operative of 550 milk producers, Parma ham by a co-operative of pig keepers on the banks of the Po.

This pattern of production is not confined to the so-called 'third Italy'. There are similar industrial regions in Denmark, Germany and the Basque and Valencian regions of Spain.

Alternatives of this kind already exist in many of the core areas of today's economy. In the face of industrialized food, Japanese consumers (almost all women) in collaboration with local farmers have created a remarkable food box scheme. Once a week they put in their orders, gather to assemble the produce into boxes and deliver them through a network of their own local micro groups (known as Han). The consumer co-ops now have 12 million members and have started associated co-ops for food processing, packaging, design, printing and catering, and are currently extending into childcare, health and elder care.

Or take renewable energy. Denmark produces a quarter of its energy from windpower. This is largely generated from turbines owned by more than 2,000 local wind co-operatives. The UK has many fewer, but those that there are can now distribute their energy through the recently formed Midcounties Co-operative Energy, which attracted 20,000 members in its first year. There are similar thriving co-operative networks in fields such as education, health, social care and sport.

Democratic decision making

Many people's idea of co-operatives is coloured by the problems that any small group of us has in choosing a place to eat, or by the idea of incessant discussions that make it hard to run anything. But in order to survive, co-ops have had to find effective means of running themselves democratically and making that involvement a source of strength, not weakness.

It is least complex at the level that evolutionary biologists say is the maximum for close personal ties. The British anthropologist and evolutionary psychologist Robin Dunbar puts this at 150. Interestingly, the largest 22 worker co-ops in the UK have an average of 41 members, with only the largest, Suma Wholefoods, reaching Dunbar's 150. If anyone doubts the viability of co-ops they should look at Suma. The staff circulate the various tasks among themselves, so each person knows the enterprise as a whole. They are a constant source of innovative ideas (and are paid equally). The key post is not the finance director but the person responsible for the staff, who would normally be called the director of human resources.

Many co-ops are much larger than this – credit unions can have millions of members – but many of them are built up from what we could call 'Dunbar cells', combined into confederations for those things that need a larger scale of operation.

The Mondragon network of worker co-ops in the Basque region of Spain exemplifies this. Its inspiration, the priest Jose Arizmendiarrieta, shared Gandhi's belief in human-scale organizations. If a Mondragon co-op got too large, he recommended it spin off some of its parts to a new co-op. Mondragon's collective services, such as its bank, are owned by the co-ops they serve, just as the local credit unions control their apex organizations. This is a widespread feature of co-operative democracy – small local units controlling the collective service organizations above them.

There are other conditions for effective democracy. First is a commitment to human-oriented technology. For Gandhi this was epitomized by the spinning wheel. His lifelong argument with Nehru was that the large-scale technology advocated by Nehru would have its own imperatives and interests and could never be subject to effective democratic control. In Mondragon, there is a commitment to modern technology (there are three large research laboratories) but it is a technology that is understood and controlled by the worker-owners.

Second, it is not just a quantitative question of one member, one vote. It is a qualitative one about the degree of a member's involvement, and his or her development as a person. Gandhi's formulation was that co-operation was an extension of the principle of self-rule or *swaraj*. He rooted the idea of co-operatives in personal and spiritual and not merely collective terms. This has been a theme of many of the major co-operative movements, secular and religious, of the past 150 years. In other words, co-ops are not merely about collective economic power but about the skills and rewards of being social. It is about the power to be human, not just the power to get more.

This helps explain the strong emphasis in co-operatives on education. The earliest co-operators, the Rochdale Pioneers, wanted to spend 10 per cent of their surplus on education but were restricted to 2.5 per cent by the Registrar of Friendly Societies. Many of the early British co-ops had a reading room and library, and a wide-ranging education programme for members. The Mondragon co-ops arose from courses run by Arizmendiarrieta, and education remains the primary pillar of the group today – it even has its own university. Arizmendiarrieta referred to this remarkable network of worker co-ops as an educational project with an economic base.

The idea of co-operative democracy is one of members individually and collectively 'in process', not the punctuated sounding out of fragmented opinion. It is about what the French sociologist Bruno Latour called 'reassembling the social', not as a concept separate and opposed to (or dominating) the individual, but rather as something created and recreated through the forms and processes of daily practice. As a result it works best when its members have a close pragmatic interest in the work of the co-op. There are lessons here that are transferable to the state.

The social sector
The early British consumer societies required members to shop only at their co-op. Each member therefore had a keen interest in the relative quality and price of its products, and how it was run. The same is true of worker and farmer co-ops, and of services such as education and healthcare that benefit from continuing relationships of trust.

The latter are areas of potential co-operative growth. There are many economic problems that involve the collaboration of different parties for their solution. In social care, for example, there are the receivers of care together with their families and neighbours, as well as the care givers and funders. New multi-stakeholder co-ops have sprung up that have led to a marked improvement in the quality of care. Quebec has been a leader in North America. In Europe it is Italy that has again been the pioneer. There are now 14,000 Italian care co-operatives. In cities such as Bologna social co-ops now provide 85 per cent of public care services.

There is a parallel trend – for similar reasons – in education. In England, there are today 405 co-operative schools. Many of them are in deprived neighbourhoods. As state schools they had been threatened with special measures and transfer to the growing number of private educational chains. Instead they have converted to co-operatives, the membership ranging from children and parents to teachers, community supporters and local colleges. The schools have established their own secondary co-op to provide the kind of support services that local authorities have been cutting and privatizing.

The threat from competitive markets

Karl Marx was in favour of co-operatives. He saw them as practice grounds for working-class people to run the economy. But he thought they would always be limited by the market competition of private capital. The productive power of capitalist technology coupled with cheap labour would always tend to destroy co-operatives or press them to follow a capitalist path. The wings of aspiration would be sharply clipped.

Today's co-operative economy reflects this continuing competition from the market. There are at least four ways in which co-ops have survived:

- Individual visionary initiatives have succeeded in areas peripheral to the main economy. These have been confined to gaps beneath the private market's radar.
- There are some co-ops that, in the face of direct mainstream

competition, have, as Marx forecast, had to match the scale and centralized structures of their private rivals (in some co-operative banking, building societies and mutual insurance, for example). They still have some of the protection of co-operative structures but member ties are weak and open to the threat of demutualization.

- In some countries co-ops have had a measure of protection against the private market via government legislation or financial support.
- Some co-ops have developed networks like those I have described, whose principles and alternative ways of working have given them decisive advantages against private competition.

Particular co-operatives may experience each of these in turn (or simultaneously). Many have started as movements of the marginalized. Some have then grown and found ways of providing services without sacrificing all the advantages of small, human-sized cells.

The successful networks have their own ecology. They collaborate on buying and selling. They raise finance from co-operative banks and share know-how, machinery and even orders. In an era when economies of system are becoming more important than economies of scale, these co-operative systems have proved more than a match for their private competitors.

Even then they will always face the contending forces of chaos and order. Fragmentation can become a weakness rather than a strength. In the face of crises, co-operatives are often pressured into centralization as a means of survival. They then lose the advantages that come from the diversity and engagement of their members. Some of the most successful networks have found ways round this – repairing the faltering units and returning them to their members.

Marx, then, took too narrow a view of the spaces that can be opened up for an alternative economy. Such spaces will always be under pressure – from the market, from the state and at times from the corrosion of co-operative values and practices internally. In these circumstances, individual co-ops will be like small craft isolated on the ocean. They need the combined strength of a fleet.

A new climate for co-operation

They need also to focus on areas where co-operation – by its very character – has qualities that private capital cannot match. We are living in a period when these areas are growing. There are intractable problems, which neither the private market nor the state in their current forms appear able to solve. In these fields mission-driven co-operatives are potentially a more effective form of enterprise than the private corporation.

In Britain, to realize this potential requires a radical strengthening of our own co-operative economy. The primacy of a broad, liberal co-operative education is a first priority. Ways need to be found to use existing co-operative strongholds as platforms for innovation and expansion into the new 'intractable' fields. At a point when ideas, knowledge and information have become the key to competitiveness, every co-operative has to find ways of tapping into the ideas of the many millions of co-operative members.

Co-operatives also have to develop new relations with the state. In the past, civic co-operation has been jealous of its autonomy, while the labour tradition has seen co-operatives as a potential threat to state services. But in many areas they are natural allies, not opponents. Each represents a way of realizing social and environmental goals. There are already examples of public/social partnerships, carefully protected against privatization. For such partnerships to work, the state will need to be innovative in its structures of finance, accountability, employment and contracting.

In the early 20th century there was a strong current among co-operators and guild socialists that recognized such a model of a civil economy and a supportive state. While it was out of tune with the era of mass production, the revolution in information technology and the internet has changed the industrial and post-industrial paradigm. It has led to a surge of informal civic co-operation. This is now a world of open source software, Creative Commons, Wikipedias. Informal co-operation has already extended far beyond the dreams of William Morris.

In the formal economy, co-operation is already well rooted. It has its own systems of management and accountability. At its best it is driven by its social rather than short-term profit imperatives. In the debris of the current financial meltdown, this reversal is what so many areas of our daily lives require. Co-operation in its many forms now has the wind behind it. It now has the capacity to expand its fleet.

Robin Murray is a Senior Visiting Fellow at the London School of Economics.

This essay first appeared in the radical UK magazine *Red Pepper* in May 2012. For more information visit redpepper.org.uk

2
Can co-operatives crowd out capitalism?

Wayne Ellwood

In the eyes of the mainstream media and the high priests of the free market, Argentina just doesn't get it. In May 2012, the country was savaged by the international business press for nationalizing the Spanish-owned oil company, YPF. Scarcely mentioned was the fact that Argentina's oil and gas industry was only 'privatized' in the late-1990s under pressure from the International Monetary Fund (IMF) and other hard-line enforcers of then fashionable neoliberal economic policies. Like many countries around the world, Argentina's oil industry used to be state-owned.

Back in 2001, the knives were out again. After years of enforced austerity and 'structural adjustment' the resource-rich South American country was awash in debt, crippling inflation, staggering unemployment and negative economic growth. (Notice any parallels with present-day Greece and Spain?) The IMF's prescription for setting the economy right – 'flexible' labour conditions, deregulation, loosening of capital controls, privatization of state-owned assets, devaluation of the national currency – only made things worse.

With inflation raging and tens of thousands of workers on the streets, the government finally called it quits, defaulting on its debt and devaluing its currency. Predictably, the kingpins of global finance went ballistic, warning that Argentina would sink into penury and chaos.

It didn't happen. Over the next decade the country's GDP grew by nearly 90 per cent, the fastest in Latin America. Poverty fell and employment rose steadily while government spending on social services slowly increased.

Many factors contributed to this astounding turnaround, including the determination of Argentineans to strike an independent economic course not reliant on the whims of foreign capital.

But a significant part of its success is rooted in Argentina's rich history of co-operatives. Waves of Jewish and Italian immigrants brought the co-operative vision with them during the early 20th century. Co-ops were well established, especially in agriculture, prior to the financial and political meltdown in 2001. According to the International Co-operative Alliance (ICA), nearly a quarter of the South American country's 40 million people are linked directly or indirectly to co-operatives and mutual societies.

So when the national economy collapsed and the country's business class started to bail out, abandoning factories and stripping assets, the workers had a better idea. They decided to form worker co-ops and run the factories themselves. The movement became known as *las empresas recuperadas* (recovered companies). You can see the background to the Argentine crisis and the story of one such takeover in Avi Lewis' and Naomi Klein's inspiring documentary, *The Take*.

It was by no means an easy road. One estimate put the number of factories around Buenos Aires abandoned by their owners at close to 4,000. Argentina was a country steeped in decades of corrupt, clientalist politics and 'I'm-all-right-Jack' trade unionism. Democratic ownership, the workers taking control, running their own factories as co-operatives, was a stretch. How to re-engineer a top-down system of traditional management where employees defer to authority in an adversarial workplace? The psychological shift alone was daunting. But desperate times can bolster resolve. Against all odds, including belligerent bosses, intransigent owners and reluctant bureaucrats, the idea took hold.

Today, there are more than 200 'recovered' co-operative factories in Argentina – up from 161 companies in 2004 – providing jobs for more than 9,000 people. Most are smallish, which means the hands-on approach is a little easier to manage. Three-quarters of the firms employ fewer than 50 workers, though two per cent have more than 200 employees. They are scattered across a range of industries from shoes and textiles to meatpacking plants and transport firms.[1]

What began as a brave experiment after the economic collapse of 2001 has become a vibrant and stable part of the economy. According to University of Buenos Aires researcher Andrés Ruggeri: 'The workers learned that running a company by themselves is a viable alternative. That was unthinkable before... These are workers who have got back on their feet on their own.'[2]

As in Argentina's 2001 crisis, the co-operative spirit often emerges when times are toughest, in the midst of economic collapse and social disintegration, when people are searching for alternatives. A little history is instructive.

Radical thinkers

Weavers formed the first documented co-operative society in 1769 in Fenwick, Scotland. But the modern co-op movement really began with the Rochdale Society of Equitable Pioneers in December 1844. As the Industrial Revolution rolled across Britain, a menacing, muscular form of capitalism was remaking the country from top to bottom. Thousands of workers lost their jobs to the new steam-powered machines; the cities were flooded with unemployed; poverty and illness soared as the skies blackened; men, women and small children worked 70 hours a week in life-threatening conditions in the booming mills and factories.

Across Europe, radical thinkers sparked opposition to the ravages of this new industrial capitalism. Proudhon, Fourier, Owen, Marx and Engels all argued for a social and political order where people would come before profit and where co-operation would trump competition. In Rochdale, a bustling mill town north of Manchester, 30 citizens, including 10 weavers, pooled their savings and opened a tiny shop selling candles, butter, sugar, flour and oatmeal. By combining forces they were able to afford basics they could not normally buy. Soon they were also selling tea and tobacco. It was a success and an inspiration that gave birth to a new movement. In the next half-century co-operatives and credit unions spread through Europe and around the globe.

According to the ICA, more than a billion people are now involved in co-operative ventures – as members, customers, employees or worker/owners. Co-operatives also provide over 100 million jobs – 20 per cent more than transnationals. There are producer, retail and consumer co-ops and they're spread across every industry. Members may benefit from cheaper prices, friendly service or better access to markets but, most importantly, the democratic structure of co-operatives means members are ultimately in charge. A core principle is 'one member, one vote'. It's that sense of control that builds social capital and makes co-operatives such a vital source of community identity. Profits might be reinvested in the business, shared among members or channelled to the local community. Because they exist to benefit their members, rather than to line the pockets of private shareholders, co-operatives are fundamentally more democratic. They empower people. They build community. They strengthen local economies.

The stunning success of the co-op movement was reason enough to celebrate 2012 as the UN's International Year of

Co-operatives. But the timing was propitious for other reasons. We're living with an economic system that is producing vast wealth for the few at the expense of the majority. The model is broken and the damage to people, communities and the natural world is growing. In the aftermath of the great financial meltdown of 2008 and the continuing instability of the global economy there is an urgent need – and a deep yearning – for balance and equality. The search for alternatives has never been more urgent. As US social critic and author Chris Hedges has written: 'The demented project of endless capitalist expansion, profligate consumption, senseless exploitation and industrial growth is now imploding.'[3]

Old orthodoxies hold firm

And so it is. But not gracefully. The owners of capital are unlikely to cede power willingly. The Occupy movement struck a powerful chord and new research underlines the notion that social ills are rooted in inequality. Income gaps weaken society and make things worse for everyone, not just the poor. 'It's what they're yearning for out there on the streets of the Occupy movement – to have some active engagement in their community and in their economy,' says Dame Pauline Green, president of the ICA. 'That's what they want.'

Yet inequality is growing almost everywhere and those in power refuse to do anything about it. In the US, where belief in free markets reigns supreme, the incomes of the richest 1 per cent of Americans grew 58 per cent from 1993-2010 while the rest rose just 6.4 per cent.

Against reason, science and empirical evidence, the old orthodoxies hold firm: 'The market will sort things out. Economic growth will be our salvation. Technology will save us.' Yet people sense there is something wrong even if they can't quite identify the problem. Middle-class budgets are stretched. Young people can't find meaningful work or affordable housing; the ranks of the poor are growing; social services are pared back while the welfare state is dismantled. People have lost faith in big government, big banks, big business, Wall Street and the City of London. Karl Marx wrote of the dislocating social upheaval of his time that 'all that is solid melts into air'. It is just as apt today.

A central part of what's missing is economic democracy. As corporate critic Marjorie Kelly notes: 'Our politics and economy are so intertwined that imbalances in wealth and ownership have eroded our political democracy. To fix this we need to democratize the economic aspect of sovereignty.'[4]

Without overstating the case, co-operatives can help do precisely that. They offer a way to democratize ownership and to counter the divisions and inequalities of the market economy. The co-op model is a challenge to the hyper-competitive, winner-takes-all model of corporate capitalism. Co-operatives show there is another way of organizing the market where profit is not the sole objective and where, theoretically, fairness is institutionalized and people are at the centre of decision-making.

But can co-ops actually 'crowd out capitalism'? University of Wisconsin sociologist Erik Olin Wright believes they can play a vital role in expanding democratic space. Co-ops help rebuild the public sphere and create a wedge between the market and the state. Wright talks of a 'symbiotic' transformation where co-ops spearhead a wider democratic surge to help bolster civil society and put down roots in the cracks of the existing system.

People over capital

Co-operatives can be a community anchor and they can revitalize the local economy. When the Fonderie de l'Aisne in Trelou sur Marne, northeast of Paris, was threatened with closure, a group of 22 former workers came up with a bold plan. They bought the factory and reopened it as a co-operative. Now they run the place themselves. The workers are 'really motivated and provide solutions to problems,' says manager Pascal Foire. 'We work for ourselves and for our own future.'

But for co-ops really to tip the balance, Wright points to

the need for some key policy changes. These include access to publicly financed credit markets at below market rates (to solve the problem of under-capitalization) and more 'cross-subsidizing and risk pooling' between co-ops themselves.

There is no question that mutual support works. The massive Mondragon Co-operative, a $23-billion global operation in Spain's Basque region, is a case in point. Of the group's 270 component companies, only one has gone out of business during the current Spanish crisis. And all these workers were absorbed by other co-ops.

Co-operative by nature

Despite Mondragon's success, we live with an economic system that is inimical to the spirit of co-operation. Competition and efficiency are its watchwords. You could even say it is systemically unco-operative, based on individuals operating in their own self-interest. The right-wing icon Ayn Rand mythologized unbridled capitalism as the pinnacle of freedom but it was Margaret Thatcher, in her attack on the 'nanny state', who put it most baldly way back in 1987 when she said 'there is no such thing as society'. Mrs Thatcher's current heir in Westminster, David Cameron, is both more cynical and more devious. His 'Big Society' formulation calls on citizens to pick up the pieces after the state withdraws from the provision of social services. Help each other because you're on your own. In the end the vision is the same.

And yet we are a supremely co-operative species by nature. How else to account for our ability to survive and prosper in every corner of this planet, from the frozen Arctic tundra to the blistering Australian outback? Harvard maths and biology professor Martin Novak describes co-operation as the 'master architect' of evolution.

Of course, reality does not always live up to theory. Co-ops operate within market structures and must rely on human beings to make them work. The competitive market is ruthless and those who can't compete are trampled underfoot. Co-operation can sometimes drift into co-optation. And people are... well, people – sometimes nasty, selfish, lazy, opinionated, bull-headed. While co-operation for mutual benefit is a good idea, the road may be bumpy.

In his recent book, *Wired for Culture*, the evolutionary biologist Mark Pagel argues that culture is made possible by social learning, which in turn depends on co-operation. Evolution allows co-operation to flourish within groups – but not necessarily between them.

'It is our uniquely human sense of social and cultural relatedness that makes our co-operation work... we are prompted to behave well toward each other; but even slightly perceived differences can end in xenophobia, racism, and extreme violence.'[5]

The same drive that pulls people together can also cause them to turn on anyone different as a perceived threat. Choose your own horror. The list is endless: Stalin's Gulag, the poisonous antisemitism in Nazi Germany, the slaughter in Rwanda, the carnage in ex-Yugoslavia. The co-operative urge, while strong and innate, does not always lead to sweetness and light. People can co-operate for bad ends as well as good. Street gangs co-operate, but so do surgical teams. Building bridges of mutual understanding and eroding both tribal and group frontiers has to be at the forefront of the co-operative vision.

A good idea takes root

Where plants are closed down, worker co-operatives can reopen them. The 'recovered factories' co-op movement is spreading in Latin America. There are 69 'recovered factories' in Brazil, around 30 in Uruguay, 20 in Paraguay and a handful in Venezuela.

We've got some endgame issues facing us as a species, problems which will require us to co-operate at a global level if we are to get through the next century without catastrophe. Climate change, resource depletion, ecological collapse and galloping consumerism: these are challenges few business or political leaders have the courage to confront. The UN itself is one chequered attempt to unite the peoples of the world in a common project of peace and prosperity. It has been fraught, to say the least.

We can no longer afford the free-market shenanigans of the past decade, the free-wheeling state-capitalist Chinese model or the dead hand of traditional communism. We will have to do much better.

Co-operatives can point the way towards a different kind of economic model, where people control capital and not the other way around.

A little real democracy wouldn't hurt.

Wayne Ellwood is a co-editor of *New Internationalist* magazine based in Toronto, Canada.

This essay first appeared in the July/August 2012 edition of *New Internationalist* magazine. For more information visit newint.org

1 *Las Empresas Recuperadas en la Argentina*, Andrés Ruggeri, Open Faculty Programme, University of Buenos Aires, 2010. **2** 'Worker-run factories in Argentina continue to thrive, boosting the economy and influencing workers in other countries', Marcela Valente, IPS, 12 November 2010. **3** 'The implosion of capitalism', Chris Hedges, *Truthdig*, 30 April 2012. **4** 'Can there be good corporations?' Marjorie Kelly, *Yes Magazine*, Spring 2012. **5** *Wired for Culture*, Mark Pagel, WW Norton 2012.

Further reading
* John Restakis, *Humanizing the Economy: co-operatives in the age of capital*, New Society Publishers, Gabriola Island, BC, 2010.
* Martin Nowak with Roger Highfield, *Super Co-operators: altruism, evolution, and why we need each other to succeed*, Free Press, New York, 2012.
* Richard Sennett, *Together: the rituals, pleasures and politics of co-operation*, Yale University Press, New Haven, 2012.
* Mark Pagel, *Wired for Culture: the natural history of human co-operation*, WW Norton, London/New York, 2012.
* David Sloan Wilson, *The Neighborhood Project*, Little, Brown & Co, New York, 2011.

3
Past, present and future
Cliff Mills

Like the search for the Holy Grail of Arthurian legend, searching for an alternative (any alternative) to capitalism might sound like the pursuit of an imaginary goal; a dream that can never be fulfilled. Nothing could be further from the truth. A co-operative alternative to capitalism was to some extent achieved in the past; but at present it eludes us. This essay seeks to understand why this is the case, and asks what we need to do to make it a real possibility for the future.

The past

Those who pioneered the establishment of co-operatives in the North of England nearly 200 years ago had already found a working alternative to capitalism. Capitalism had failed, and was failing them. It did not provide them with access to basic goods and services, because what they bought was contaminated, poor quality and over-priced, and they had no alternative source of supply. There was a market failure and an alternative was needed. Capitalism did not actually help those it claimed to serve.

The early co-operators found a mechanism through which ordinary people, by pooling their need for something and acting collectively, could meet their most basic requirements, and those of their families and communities. Driven by poverty and hunger, they were motivated by the simple need to find the solution themselves – self-help, because nobody else was going to do it for them.

The co-operative way of trading that they established provided them with an alternative to businesses owned by private commercial interests and trading for private benefit. It was an alternative way of doing business; it was an alternative way of funding business; and it was actually a basis for a different economy and a different way of living.

It was an alternative way of doing business, because its starting point was not the same as privately owned businesses, which is to generate a financial reward for the owner of the business: co-operative purpose was to provide access to goods and services on a fair and sustainable basis. Anybody could become a member, and all members had an equal voice in members' meetings and in electing their representatives who were responsible for running the business. But because its purpose was not to maximize profitability, there was no need to charge customers a mark-up on the cost. Goods could be sold on the basis of cost, plus the overheads which needed to be built into the price to enable the business to support itself, and an appropriate contingency to enable the business to protect itself against unforeseen risks.

By definition, its selling prices would be lower than those of an investor-owned business, which would additionally charge an owner's mark-up to generate a reward or profit for investors. The co-operative business did not need to do this. It had to be profitable – that is to say, its income needed to exceed its expenditure, because otherwise it would make a loss and ultimately fail. But because its purpose was to provide access to goods and services on a fair and sustainable basis, it merely had to cover its costs, overheads and contingencies. If those contingencies did not materialize, then it could redistribute or give back the money, or some of it, to customers in proportion to what they had bought (the co-operative dividend).

This was a fundamentally different way of doing business because it was not funded by investors. In the days before the existence of high-street financial services, those fortunate enough to have some cash left at the end of the week either had to keep it on them, or leave it at home when they went out to work. Through withdrawable share capital (a bit like a building society account in Britain today) co-operative shops provided a convenient place for people to store the cash for which they did not have an immediate need. Members benefited from this security, and the ability to leave their dividend in their account until it was needed.

As one of the conditions of membership, members were required to keep a minimum amount in their share account, which could be built up over time. The cash deposited by members provided working capital for the business. Under co-operative principles, minimal interest if any was paid on capital because the primary mechanism for distribution (redistribution) of any surplus which the business did not need was to customers on the basis of their trade with the society, not as a return on capital. So co-operative capital did not seek a reward – it was not greedy. The benefit was in having the local business providing access to goods and services on a fair and sustainable basis. For members, a secure place to store cash was an added bonus.

It was a basis for a different economy and a different way of living because, although it was based on self-help and self-interest, it only worked if the community collectively committed itself to the business and remained loyal. By and large, they did, and it was an idea that grew rapidly as the capital base for the movement steadily increased. It was collective self-help, which required individuals to commit themselves to the well-being of their wider community (the common interest) in order to meet their own personal needs.

If an individual was dissatisfied as a customer, their responsibility was to make their complaint known and use their rights as a member (access to elected representative, ability to attend a members' meeting, ability to seek election) to get the business to change and improve. We would say today that co-operatives were driven by a strong mechanism of accountability, which members had every incentive to use in order to preserve their local services and their own financial security.

Not only did this way of doing business produce efficient, highly customer-focused enterprises that grew steadily, it also engendered a wider sense of responsibility or citizenship – people were prepared to take action to improve things for their own well-being and that of their community. The DNA of these organizations was mutual self-help, because that was how people met their own needs. So, through the surplus generated by trade, rather than distribute it all as dividends, co-operative societies became the early providers of what we today think of as public services: access to books and newspapers, education and learning, cultural and recreational activities. It was for the members to decide how to use the surplus at the end of the year and whether to spend it in this way. So this different way of doing business engendered a different way of living, a different type of society, which cared for the more vulnerable and for those who might be disadvantaged. It is no accident that co-operatives were ahead of their time in terms of social reform, such as providing equal voting rights to women and men, allowing women to sign for their dividend, recognizing a minimum wage 90 years before UK legislation, and other areas including pensions and working conditions.

So much for the past: the co-operative way of trading worked. Co-operatives were providing an alternative to capitalism. They provided people with access to goods and services; they provided employment; and they provided a safe place for people to keep their money.

The decline

By the 1960s, co-operative retailing accounted for over 30 per cent of the food market in the UK, similar to Tesco's market share today. But the rest of the 20th century was a sad story of decline, as the large supermarkets grew rapidly, fuelled by increasing mobility, growing consumer choice, offering better quality, greater efficiency, and providing financial incentives for executives such as share options that co-operatives could not offer. Aggressive competition from new forms of capitalism, principally the public limited company and ready access to capital through a listing on the London Stock Exchange, saw co-operative retailing go through a long period of decline.

The second half of the 20th century also witnessed the decline of other parts of the traditional mutual movement. The introduction of the welfare state in 1948 replaced a great deal of mutual and co-operative provision, particularly social security provided by friendly societies. Although the emerging public sector owed much in terms of its ethos and indeed its workforce to the mutual self-help movement and, of course, to the philanthropic sector which were its forerunners, it largely marginalized them in the process.

The race for scale and volume also saw the loss of over 70 per cent of the building-society movement, as individual societies converted into banks. Promoted at the time as the only way to enable building societies to compete with the publicly listed banks, with their access to the capital markets, the reality is that while managers enjoyed large increases in remuneration, none of the demutualized building societies survived: they have all since either failed or been taken over by foreign institutions.

Why was so much in terms of capital assets and market share built up over 100 years or so, lost in less than 50 years? It was not that the idea of co-operation or mutual self-help had failed; it just no longer seemed to resonate with the contemporary world. Growing prosperity, increasing mobility, belief in 'the market', and a culture of individualism that saw the pursuit of private ownership and personal goals as the norm – this was the age of consumerism. There no longer seemed to be a problem to which collective self-help provided a solution. Why did you have to join something to buy food or insurance?

Co-operation wasn't broken – it had just been overtaken by events, and made irrelevant by a culture in which doing things collectively for a shared or common good no longer seemed to resonate. There seemed to be no point in being a co-operative in an individualistic and consumerist society. Private investor-ownership was clearly the answer, and was now both the unchallenged model of business and the foundation of economic thinking for the future. And in areas where the private sector did not operate, then the rapidly expanding welfare state would provide public services paid for through central taxation.

The recovery

The decline did not last long. In historical terms, it was a short gap between 1989, which was perhaps the high-point of self-confidence and belief that, in capitalism, Western civilization had found its Holy Grail, and 2007, when things started to go seriously wrong. Before the onset of the financial crises which proceeded to engulf this economy amongst many others, the UK co-operative movement had embarked on a long overdue process of introspection. This resulted in a blunt wake-up call from the Co-operative Commission, whose report 'The Co-operative Advantage' pulled no punches in describing how the movement had both lost its way commercially and lost sight of its social goals. Set up by the Prime Minister, Tony Blair, in 2000, the Commission proclaimed the need for the movement to rediscover its very reason for existence. It needed to re-establish the Co-operative Advantage through improved commercial performance, to enable it to pursue and deliver social goals, which would itself drive the competitive advantage.

Much has been achieved since the Commission's report was published in 2001. Although the co-operative share of the food market had declined further to less than five per cent (and dropping) by 2005, the decline was stopped and reversed through a series of co-operative mergers and acquisitions, a development of the Co-operative brand, a much more unified trading platform, and the growth of membership and the profile of membership within co-operative retailing.

There was also a surge of growth in community-based initiatives, supported both by Co-operatives UK and the Co-operative Foundation. Other initiatives, exploring how co-operative and mutual ideas could be used once more in the delivery of public services, became established. These included social housing from 2001 (Community Housing Mutual, Community Gateway); NHS Foundation Trusts from 2003, as a key element of National Health Service reform; and co-operative trust schools from 2008. Much changed in the first decade of the new century.

But the biggest boost to co-operative and mutual fortunes has been caused by events outside the movement, namely the financial crises since 2007. The public limited company, which seemed to have become widely accepted as the way of the future, suddenly appeared to be open to question. The way in which the banks had behaved over recent years, resulting in massive public bail-outs; the phone-hacking scandal and closure of *The News of the World* newspaper; the way public limited companies had behaved and treated the public, customers and employees: all of these played a big part in changing the dynamic. Outrage over executive remuneration, bankers' bonuses and tax avoidance, highlighted by protesters including UK Uncut and the Occupy movement, have further highlighted cynical practices and gross inequality. All of this has undermined public trust and confidence in big business.

But in spite of all this, we still cannot argue today that there is a co-operative alternative to capitalism. Notwithstanding the collapse of confidence and damage to the reputation of traditional capitalism on the one hand, and the revival in the fortunes of co-operative and mutual businesses on the other, in truth not much has changed. Co-operative ideas seem to have been unable to seize the moment. Why is this?

Because, I believe, modern co-operatives have not found a way of getting access to capital in the modern world. This needs to be explained.

In Rochdale in 1844, for many people the co-operative store provided the only safe place to keep cash. Crucially, it also provided the business with access capital at negligible cost. Co-operative capital was not profit-seeking or greedy; it was 'disinterested' because the point of the exercise (the corporate purpose, and members' aspiration) was access to goods and services on a fair and sustainable basis. Members were happy to deposit their spare cash without any expectation of interest because, before high-street financial services became available, they knew nothing else.

The situation today is very different. With cash machines, internet banking and a plethora of providers of financial services and products, there are many other ways of managing your cash, and of storing or building up funds for retirement. Everybody looks for whatever will give them the best deal or the highest return. Capital today is profit-seeking and greedy: it wants the highest return.

The harsh reality today is that we are all addicted to the idea of profit maximization. Who would not seek to get the highest return on any spare money which was not needed for today? It is not just businesses – and in particular large businesses – that are driven by the need to generate profits for shareholders rather than to promote the public good. We are all now caught up in a culture which sees this as normal. We live in a society that views the accumulation of private wealth and prosperity as every person's assumed agenda; it expects us to behave as 'consumers', shopping for the best and most convenient deal for us, without regard for the consequences; as workers, looking for the maximum remuneration and then bound into organizations intent on growth and competition to maximize their profitability; and, as savers, looking for the highest return on our investment.

The maximization of profit and the pursuit of private gain are now socially acceptable and have become thoroughly institutionalized in modern society. The modern world is dominated by businesses designed to maximize profitability rather than the public good because that is what we as individuals are seeking. We want gain.

In that context, co-operative capital is not what people are looking for. So, with a small number of exceptions, modern co-operative societies no longer fund their businesses using withdrawable co-operative share capital. Not only is it not an attractive option for members, but having to process such financial transactions at the check-out is more complex in the modern regulated environment, and withdrawable share capital no longer looks like a sensible basis for funding a business. So the large retail co-operatives are funded mainly by accumulated reserves and commercial borrowing.

For the present, there may be a great desire for new co-operative businesses to be created in the UK and elsewhere, but in practice there is a major factor holding this back, and that factor is access to capital. The money is out there, but because its owners are chasing profits, they are not interested in co-operative capital. Meanwhile, subject to a continuing bumpy ride, capitalism marches on, with new flotations like Facebook and raising money on existing businesses. In 2011, some £23 billion ($37 billion) was raised on the London Stock Exchange by new companies coming to the market, or by existing companies raising further finance.

The number of co-operatives may be increasing, but not on this scale. Even the coalition government in the UK, in spite of its efforts to promote the mutualization of public services, has only been able to deliver small-scale results. There is lots of relatively small-scale activity, and the larger businesses emerging from the public sector in the main are asset-light, and so don't need large amounts of capital. They are hoping to build it up through trading over the coming years because there is no current mechanism for such businesses to attract new capital.

So at present there is no imminent prospect of a co-operative alternative to capitalism. The pursuit of private gain is too deeply embedded. The problem now is us: the patterns of our economic behaviour determine the world we live in, and collectively we are choosing profit. Until we change, and co-operative capital once again becomes as attractive as profit-seeking capital, co-operatives will never be able to play in the same league. Is that ever going to happen?

The future

This is really a fundamental question about human nature, and the instinct of the species for survival. If capitalism is destroying the planet, at what point will humanity realize that its addiction to the pursuit of gain will ultimately bring about its destruction? With the combination of limited natural resources, a growing world population, and a global economy whose engine is growth based on the pursuit of private gain, only one outcome is likely. If you factor in the availability of weapons of mass destruction, and governments largely beholden to business interests, the future looks fragile.

But the future really is in our hands. In the 21st century, available capital is largely tied up in shares in profit-maximizing businesses. A large portion of the money we save for our retirement and the money we pay for all manner of insurance premiums and numerous other financial products and services is stored or invested in places where those making decisions about where to invest it think it will make the highest possible return. This is the professional world of investment, where small sums from a myriad of different sources are aggregated into very large sums which are managed by those watching market behaviours, studying social, political and economic developments, and making assumptions to predict where to place our funds to secure the best return.

The capital that businesses need already exists. As the minister says when addressing the congregation on launching the appeal for funds to mend the church roof: 'The good news is that we already have the money we need. The bad news is that it is still in your pockets.' The capital needed to fund a co-operative economy exists. In industrializing Britain in the 19th century, it was in people's pockets, under the bed, and in other places where it was not productive. Today, it is too busy chasing profit.

If we really crave a different world, then the solution is in our own hands, because those who manage our funds are doing what we want them to do: give us the highest return. If we want something different, then we need to ask for it. This is where the fundamental question about human nature arises. Are people ever likely to do anything other than try to get the best and the most they can for themselves? Is it not the case that humans are selfish, competitive, greedy and self-interested?

This has been the assumption of economists for decades, and is the foundation on which modern economic theory is based. It is the basis on which economists predict future behaviour, and of the assumptions they use in modelling economic outcomes. But, in recent years, this has become subject to challenge, by evolutionary scientists, by anthropologists and by political scientists. The recent financial meltdown has also caused many more to doubt whether the historic assumptions were ever right.

Elinor Ostrom, who won the 2009 Nobel Prize in Economics following the financial collapse, found in her research that co-operation is often key to managing common resources successfully.[1] According to the Nobel committee, she 'challenged the conventional wisdom that common property is poorly managed and should be either regulated by central authorities or privatized'.[2] In her Prize Lecture, she said: 'The most important lesson for public policy analysis, derived from the intellectual journey I have outlined here, is that humans have a more complex motivational structure and more capability to solve social dilemmas than posited in earlier rational-choice theory. Designing institutions to force (or nudge) entirely self-interested individuals to achieve better outcomes has been the major goal posited by policy analysts for governments to accomplish for much of the last century. Extensive empirical research leads me to argue that, instead, a core goal of public policy should be to facilitate the developments of institutions that bring out the best in humans.'

David Sloan Wilson, professor of biology and anthropology, believes in the concept of co-operative evolution based on natural selection at a group level, both within and between groups. At the Co-operative Opportunity Conference in London in February 2012, he said: 'Is it any wonder that we have produced countless business leaders, financiers and politicians for whom the selfish pursuit of self-interest is a natural law and a maxim to live by? The truth is that individuals can evolve to behave for the good of their groups and that co-operation is the signature adaptation of our own species.'[3]

Our response

But what has that got to do with you and me? If we want a different world, a different economy, a different way of living, what can we do about it?

As an individual, there are three essential areas of direct economic activity in which I am involved, where my actions can make a difference. The first is where and from whom I buy goods and services. I can choose positively to buy from sustainable sources, to shun objectionable suppliers or sources, to spend my money locally to minimize food miles, and to support businesses that trade for a wider community benefit, rather than simply for private benefit. There are increasingly opportunities for choice, certainly in the UK, but they are limited to certain areas and sectors, and they are also limited if I am on a very low budget. Subject to that, I can do my bit. The volume of fairly traded goods is growing, co-operative retailing has stopped its decline and is now starting to grow again, and there is lots going on at grassroots level and within communities. But in the context of overall UK trade, it remains small.

The second area is where and how I earn my money: who I work for. For many people, the choices are likely to be much more limited. Large public limited companies employ a lot of people and constitute a large part of the economy. If I don't like the way my employer conducts its affairs, or the fact that it trades on the basis of narrow private benefit, it may be difficult or impossible for me to find a comparable job working for an organization which exists and trades for a wider public purpose. The continuing privatization of public services continues to reduce the opportunities for people to work for organizations other than those trading to maximize private benefit.

There is, however, also a growing number of 'social enterprises' or businesses trading for a social purpose, and a strong and vibrant movement for local businesses, Transition Towns etc, and these will create some new opportunities. But once again it is small-scale in terms of the overall jobs market.

But it is the third area of economic activity which is probably the most significant and where I have practically no choice: where I save or store my money for the future. If I had lived 150 years ago, I could have deposited it at my local co-operative store: it would have been safe; it would have supported a business providing local goods and services, at fair prices; and it would have helped to generate other public benefits for my community. I might even have earned small amounts of interest, though I might not. But I would have been happy with that because it met my aspiration for access to goods and services. I was not chasing a return on investment. This was the co-operative economy and at that time it provided a genuine alternative to capitalism, because people were not addicted to the pursuit of gain (it was not an option available to them). They were happy for their spare capital to be used to fund business on a 'disinterested' basis; it provided them with access to goods and services, and it created jobs. It worked as an economic model at that time.

But it does not work today. I can no longer save or deposit my cash like that, so how can I save 'co-operatively'? What financial products are available which would enable me to save prudently for retirement, but which would support the development of a co-operative economy, rather than the current economy that I would like to change? The answer is that there is little or nothing that is readily available. There are of course ethical funds, but these merely provide for an investment policy which avoids certain types of businesses such as arms trade, or tobacco. They still invest in profit-maximizing companies.

There is basically a gap, or more likely a gaping hole. I might like to place my retirement savings, or a portion of them, for the next 15 years (say) with an organization which traded on a co-operative basis, preferably somewhere near to where I live so that I can support it with my custom, whose annual meeting I could attend if I wanted to hear more about what it was doing and how it was meeting its business and social goals, where I could ask a question if I wanted to, and have a vote for some sort of representation in the governance – but I cannot do it.

I can invest in any number of public limited companies, because there is a widely known device that is common to all of them, and which we all know and understand (it can go down as well as up in value) and that is the corner-stone of the whole edifice: a company share. But I am not attracted to the company share and that whole edifice because it is designed to do what I don't want it to do. I don't want a system which exists merely for private interest. Of course I want my money to be reasonably safe (though there is no such thing as completely safe), and if possible I would like to receive some compensation from the business for having access to my money, but I am happy for my interests to be balanced with those of employees, customers, the local community and future generations. I want to support fairness and sustainability: not shareholder primacy.

The problem for the co-operative world today is that it does not have something comparable to the company share, which it can hold up and say – use this for your savings, and help to secure an alternative future. It is my personal view that we will have such an instrument in the near future, and that this is an essential piece of the jigsaw, but there will not be any significant take-up of such a way of saving, and we will not see the growth of a different sort of business and a different sort of economy unless we are prepared to be weaned off our addiction to the pursuit of gain. That's why the solution is in our hands.

Are we and others likely to pursue this solution?

We are talking about a movement – a popular movement for change. In reality, it has already started, with the re-awakening of interest in traditional co-operative organizations, in the social enterprise movement, the Transition Town movement, and many other locally based initiatives to challenge conventional profit-maximizing businesses. We see the sharp end of it in Los Indignados, the Occupy movement and UK Uncut. But this is still not enough unless large numbers of us are prepared to start behaving differently in relation to how we save and store our money. We need the capital instruments for this, we need the businesses trading for a wider social purpose rather than for private benefit which will attract this sort of capital, and we need a level of popular understanding and awareness to make it the norm, rather than something obscure.

This is an enormous cultural change for the business world.

It is something that could only happen gradually, and would take many years, but will it ever happen? The answer probably lies in understanding better how people behave. We have a great deal to learn still about human motivation, but consider the following:

1 Over 6 million people in the UK are informal carers, looking after friends or relatives.[4]

2 In 2009, NHS Blood and Transplant had around 1.4 million registered blood donors donating close to 2 million units of blood.[5]

3 Over 300,000 people volunteer as school governors in England.[6]

4 Over 100,000 people volunteer in hospices across the UK, and two-thirds of the costs of hospice care are covered by local fundraising.[7]

5 In August 2012, Wikipedia had 33,372 Active (volunteer) Editors for the English language, who made 5 or more edits in a month; it had 3,483 Very Active Editors who made 100 or more edits in a month.[8]

6 In 2010/11, almost 6 in every 10 adults donated to charitable causes, equivalent to 29.5 million people, and the best estimate of the total amount donated to charity by adults is £11 billion ($18 billion).[9]

7 In 2010, 17.5 million people in the UK were active practitioners of faith groups, 25 million were members of building societies, 10.3 million were members of co-operatives, 8.5 million were members of financial mutuals or friendly societies.[10]

There is some reason why humans will do things that are not just for their own personal needs or gratification, and this instinct is not limited to a saintly few. There is something fundamental in human nature which causes lots of people to do things not just for their own benefit, and to have regard for the wider needs of people.

For 200 years, capitalism has been the engine of the world's economies, fuelled by that most powerful of human instincts –

the desire for more. But something else is needed today, and our growing understanding of human nature suggests that there is hope: something else is possible.

Is there really any alternative to co-operation?

Cliff Mills is a co-operative lawyer.

1 Elinor Ostrom, 'A General Framework for Analyzing the Sustainability of Social-Ecological Systems', *Science*, 325(5939), 419-422, 2009; Xavier Basurto and Elinor Ostrom, 'Beyond the Tragedy of the Commons', *Economia delle fonti di energia e dell'ambiente*, 52(1), 35-60, 2009. 2 Royal Swedish Academy of Sciences Press Release, 12 October 2009. 3 *Co-operative News*, 16 February 2012. 4 Carers UK & University of Leeds, *Valuing carers*, 2011. 5 NHS Blood and Transplant, Annual review 2009/10, 2009. 6 National Governors Association nga.org.uk/About-Us. aspx, 2001. 7 Help the Hospices, 2012, nin.tl/178bBTY. 8 Wikipedia, 2012, nin. tl/13KHKuC, 2012. 9 NCVO, UK Giving 2011, Key findings, 2011. 10 NCVO, NCVO UK Civil Society Almanac 2012, nin.tl/178chsq

A new co-operative economy

4
Towards a new economy based on co-operation

Dan Gregory

If it is true that it is 'easier to imagine the end of the world than the end of capitalism',[1] then the question 'Is there a co-operative alternative to capitalism?' is one of the hardest to answer in the world. But perhaps, with the kind of perverse logic in which the 'popularizer' of this remark, Slavoj Žižek, himself indulges, the truth of this statement was diluted just as it was uttered: for in admitting even the faintest possibility of an alternative, this rendered it at least imaginable.

Subsequently, and rather suddenly it seems, this possibility of an alternative to capitalism has become easier to imagine. Putting aside, at least temporarily, the views of those who have long advocated other models for organizing our productive forces, a range of evidence suggests that, after many decades of 'actually existing capitalism', this model is presently failing to deliver, even on its own terms.

A failing model
First, capitalism is failing to deliver for many of the nation states in which it has been longest established on its core promises of

growth, employment, returns to capital, material security and stability. For many, growth has turned from an expectation into a memory; unemployment is at record levels in many European economies; capital's investment propositions are so insufficiently convincing that even the negative returns offered by German Federal bonds are oversubscribed; and financial collapse was only recently averted.

Second, the negative externalities which the market mechanism generates are now frighteningly large – and seemingly growing. Inequality continues to rise in the UK and further afield; the riots of 2011 bear witness to bubbling social tensions; environmental uncertainty, child poverty and mental-health problems are not going away and, if anything, are increasingly worrying. Over 40 per cent of the economy now falls under the command and control of the public sector, funded mainly through taxation, in a seemingly hopeless attempt to mitigate the social and environmental fallout of market failure.[2]

So while public interventions can crowd out private enterprise and may be obstructing the market's ability to deliver jobs and growth, there are few, if any, credible voices suggesting that, if the state just got out the way, the market alone would somehow begin to correct its own environmental and socially destructive tendencies. We are damned if we do and damned if we don't. We can't leave it to the market alone to deliver social and economic well-being but neither have we found an effective way to step in and pick up the pieces through public interventions. At best, then, our capitalist system is operating at 60-per-cent efficiency.

In this light, it is revealing that the net value of both the public and private sectors is actually negative![3] Businesses and the government both owe more than they own. Even with the vast and unprecedented financial underpinning by the state of recent years, the private sector alone is now officially worth less than nothing. We seem to have descended into a destructive duel between the public and private, fighting to stand on each other's shoulders and all the time sinking together lower into the mud. We have stumbled into a kind of accidental state capitalism, which combines, on the one hand, a monstrous version of John Maynard Keynes' interventionist state, clumsily interfering for longer and to a greater degree than he would have ever envisaged, and, on the other, a pathetic mutation of Friedrich Hayek's invisible hand, which, despite its pervasive reach into the public and social spheres, is now failing to deliver the goods. At this rate, Keynes' quip that 'in the long term we're all dead' looks optimistic.

Finally, returning to those who object to the capitalist system of production *per se*, the moral objections against it appear to be gaining ever wider support, as public disgust with bankers and bonuses becomes the norm, and as the commodification of social relationships and a reliance on a consumerist model is brought into question.

What's going wrong?

An investigation which seeks out an alternative to capitalism must inevitably begin in the private sector. What exactly seems to be the problem?

First, private enterprise does not appear to be delivering the returns that capitalism expects, with, for example, returns for venture-capital funds since the dotcom bubble close to zero.[4] Private-sector growth is low or negative in many Western economies despite historically absurdly low interest rates. Many are starting to believe that the growth we assumed was normal over the past few decades was built on an unsustainable bubble of housing, debt and the trickery of financialization.

Second, the free market is not very free. The competitive drive of the private sector which should move the invisible hand and prompt the effective allocation of scarce resources does not appear to be functioning in a very competitive way. The increasing workload of the Competition Commission[5] and the dominance by a handful of businesses of our food retail, banking and energy sectors demonstrates the increasing concentration of ownership in the private sector, the presence of oligopolies, barriers to entry, and the stifling of new enterprise and diversity.

Third, private businesses' increasingly narrow and short-term focus on a single, financial bottom line logically results in a corresponding rise in externalities. The increasing demands on central and local government, whether bailing out banks or providing welfare, are testament to the extent to which these externalities are frequently negative.

Fourth, finally and perhaps most frighteningly, despite the signals, we don't really know whether or not the private sector is failing, as our economic dashboard has become disconnected from our vehicle. We have coasted blindly into a bewildering landscape of economic post-modernism where value is always on the surface, is always negotiated, often through secondary and tertiary markets where the multiplication of intermediaries has ruptured the connections between signifier and signified. It is often near impossible for a lay person to decode quarterly financial statements; interest rates don't reflect actual lending rates; much of our national infrastructure is not included in the national accounts; trillions of pounds' worth of contingent liabilities are hidden; and copy produced by PR executives for press notices often bear little relation to the underlying economic conditions.

This schism between reality and rhetoric endangers our well-being as we do not have, either collectively or individually, any real certainty as to what's really happening in the productive economy. It is as if Wile E Coyote were wearing virtual reality headgear, oblivious to whether he is on safe ground, hovering over the abyss or already plunging downwards. As far as we know, we may be close to the point of doing irrevocable damage to the economy and the planet while the numbers on the screen flash a reassuring green. Or, indeed, a more ominous red. Who knows what's really behind them?

So is it possible that a co-operative model could offer us

remedies to each of these maladies? Is it possible that 'where the invisible hand fails, the handshake may succeed'?[6]

Advantages of the co-operative model

First, co-operatives and social enterprise that eschew conventional capitalist forms of ownership, perversely, have been financially outperforming red-blooded businesses within their own capitalist game. In the UK, the co-operative sector grew by more than 25 per cent between 2008 and 2011;[7] social enterprises are 'flouting the fiscal gloom to grow faster than the rest of the UK economy';[8] social enterprises are outstripping SMEs (small and medium enterprises) in terms of growth, business confidence and innovation;[9] and Spanish co-operatives saw an increase in employment by an average of 7.2 per cent in the last quarter of 2011, despite wider unemployment at record levels. Furthermore, co-operatives have higher resilience in economic crises, based on research by Roelants and Bajo.[10]

Second, co-operatives can offer two solutions to the anti-competitive conundrum. On the one hand, their ownership is intrinsically less opposed to their own subdivision into smaller units: subsidiarity and democracy lie at the heart of the co-operative model. Equally, many co-operatives and social enterprises provide a defence against takeovers and conglomeration through an asset lock, democratic ownership or disallowing dividends. On the other hand, co-operatives can sidestep the anti-competitive problem by turning such behaviour into a virtue! Co-operation and collusion are of course two sides of the same coin. Observing from a distance the assumption in the Competition Act, in EU law and inside the Competition Commission that being anti-competitive is a bad thing reveals policymakers', economists' and regulators' blinkers. Co-operatives are bound by their principles to co-operate for public benefit rather than collude for private interest. This enables us to imagine a world other than the inhuman one into which we have stumbled where co-operation – let's spell that out: 'working together' – is an illegitimate and illegal activity.

Third, co-operatives and social enterprises are set up with a responsibility to worry more about the externalities of their trading activity. Their wider obligations beyond the purely financial offer the promise of a less crass and rampant capitalism and, instead, a more humanized economy in which businesses price in the environmental and social costs. As suggested by the financial performance of co-operatives, this can actually represent a business advantage, rather than a hit on the financial bottom line, as co-operatives capture loyalty and attract trust, for example. Even if this were not true, and internalizing social and environmental costs did mean sacrificing a few percentage points on return to capital, there is a great deal of wiggle room between single digit returns and minus 40 per cent (see above).

Fourth, the co-operative model provides an exit route from the pointless (or, worse, dangerous) dead end of postmodern economics, not by retreating to traditional models but through turning to each other. Under co-operative ownership, financiers and owners *are also* the consumers or producers. As one and the same, or as peers, they are therefore connected in a more meaningful way than, say, the relationship between a supermarket shopper in the East Midlands and a trader's spreadsheet in Boston. The existence of these more direct and authentic connections can avert the dangers of distance and dislocation by re-establishing more concrete relationships between the constituent components of the economy. Furthermore, under the co-operative model, as the motivations of producers, owners and consumers are held more in common, the incentives to manipulate 'signifiers' to misrepresent the underlying economic 'signified' are fewer, reintroducing a more meaningful and transparent relationship between economic indicators and the real economy.

A new co-operative economy

What might this mean in practice if we decided to pursue a transition towards a more co-operative market economy? It could mean, for example:

- The creation of more phone, water, energy and other utility companies along co-operative lines in order to reconnect the incentives between customers and financiers;
- The further spread of community-owned shops and pubs to show the large retail chains how real engagement with customers can deliver diversity and remarkably successful financial performance (only three per cent of community shops to open have ever closed);[11]
- The appointment of more lay people, charity representatives, customers and other stakeholders on the boards of banks in order to bring a dose of realism and humanity to the governance of our financial institutions;
- The takeover of football clubs by supporters' trusts in order to bring ownership to the people who have the greatest vested interest in clubs' success;
- Consumer co-operatives running rail franchises, creating better incentives for owners as customers;
- The transformation of the Port of Dover into a so-called 'People's Port' through a community trust model;
- Customers moving their money from the handful of financial giants to mutuals, co-operatives or credit unions so as to create a more sensible financial system focused on both the longer term and the real economy.

But the failures of actually existing capitalism rest as much with the public sector as with the private. Markets are rarely truly free: the state sets the rules, offers subsidies, provides revenue, investment, taxes and tax breaks that create the playing field and can distort markets. If the state had been able to find a way to effectively harness and steer the private sector, without weighing so heavily on its back as fatally to compromise its horsepower, and used a proportion of the winnings to tidy up the mess left behind, then capitalism would be clearing the fences. Yet successive governments in the UK and across Western capitalist economies have fallen at every hurdle. But could co-operative principles help the public sector play a more constructive role within the capitalist model?

There are three conventional levers at the disposal of policymakers to correct market failure in pursuit of any given policy objective: spending, taxation and regulation. Both taxation and regulatory interventions could be more intelligently constructed in order to create a more co-operative relationship between the state and the private sector, working with business to incentivize the reduction of negative externalities in order to achieve policy goals in return for fiscal or regulatory rewards. By going beyond the conventional black-and-white policy choice of taxing or regulating either more or less, and instead using shades of grey to bring an increasing tax or regulatory burden only on those businesses which fail to pursue desired behaviours, the state can bring about the development of a private sector that is both less burdened by taxation and regulation while at the same time making a greater contribution to social and environmental, as well as economic, prosperity.

Again, what would this mean in practice? We can already see how this works in the environmental sphere through, for example, the state coming down more heavily on those businesses which emit a greater level of CO_2. The idea that this model might be improved upon and extended to the social sphere is not so far-fetched: the UK government, for example, has recently floated the possibility of relaxing health and safety regulation for those businesses with a strong track record of compliance. If this model could be extended to areas such as employment of the long-term jobless, training, research and development, and working with local communities, then this could represent an evolution toward a more liberal and proportionate state: one that links rights and responsibilities, and that rewards good corporate behaviour rather than clumsily burdening all businesses with blanket state interference.

For example, tax breaks for investors could be tweaked to provide greater relief for enterprising activities that alleviate poverty, support environmental objectives, or create jobs for NEETs (young people not in employment, education or training). Relief would be reduced for trade in tobacco, fast food and other less socially useful sectors and, overall, the net corporate tax burden would not change in the short term while decreasing in the longer term as corporate behaviour started to shift.

A co-operative public sector

Public services have conventionally been delivered either in-house by public servants within the bosom of the state or put out to competition to be delivered by the most convincing bidder, often from the private sector. Yet there are significant flaws with both models.

Evidence against the statist model can be found where teachers, nurses and other public servants have entered their profession with a commitment to making a difference and have subsequently been ground down by bureaucracy, paperwork, endless policy reversals and organizational upheaval. For others, their passion may have been dampened as they have become accustomed to job security, pensions and habit. Furthermore, public budget holders have few incentives to reduce costs and consequently can indulge in a ludicrous and shameful annual rush to get money 'out of the door' by the end of the financial year in order to justify and protect their budgets from one year to the next.

The alternatives of 'privatization', 'marketization' or 'commercialization' are no less scandalous. Take the way in which departmental and local silos institutionalize waste. EU law, for example, explicitly states that a commissioning authority is not allowed to take into account wider policy objectives in contracts where they are 'not relevant'. In practice, this means it is understood to be practically illegal for a commissioner of hospital equipment, for instance, to specify that the manufacture of this equipment should engage people far from the labour market. In addition, dissatisfaction with the commissioning process in sectors as diverse as the voluntary sector and the architectural profession – evident in their own specialist journals[12] – demonstrates another failure of public markets. This is not unjustified whingeing. Often hundreds of architectural practices bid for the same single contract. In eastern England, meanwhile, one charity estimated that it took them hundreds of hours of staff time to bid for a contract to deliver children's services that they failed to secure. By multiplying that time wasted by the number of bidders, and then again across hundreds of local authorities, and again across dozens of service areas, we can start to get a sense of the immense scale of waste. Even worse, billions of pounds are subsequently absorbed by contractual negotiations, legal fees, the establishment and maintenance of targets, monitoring, inspection and reporting regimes. Finally, perverse incentives are contractually enshrined as providers of services are under compulsion to compete with each other and are even disallowed from working across geographical and institutional boundaries in support of citizens.

So is there a co-operative alternative? The rhetoric, if not the reality, of the cross-party enthusiasm for such a model suggests there is, with Labour's *Co-operative Councils* initiative and Francis Maude's *Mutuals Programme*. In practice, neither initiative has made any significant advances into the bipolar territory ruled over by cultural, technical and legal assumptions of only in-house and outsourced options. For human resources staff in Foundation Trusts, for procurement professionals in local authorities and for strategic policymakers in central government, the conventional levers with which they are familiar remain 'command and control' versus 'compete and contest'. It is rare to find any guidance on how to co-operate and collaborate in the rule book, the Human Resources handbook and the commissioning textbook.

Yet there are several examples where a co-operative alternative has been pursued. Andrew Laird and Jessie Cunnett of the consultancy group Mutual Ventures describe how local authorities can take 'a more proactive "market-making" approach and engage with local organizations to bring potential providers together... by and large, these organizations would rather come together in collaboration than be forced into winner-takes-all competition with each other.' Similarly, under the former UK government's 'Right to Request' policy, hundreds of community health service contracts worth almost a billion pounds annually were 'spun out' into new employee-owned mutual and social enterprises with an uncontested initial contract. We could imagine more service users co-operatively owning organizations that deliver public services, each with a legal obligation to pursue the common interest.

So there is an alternative. But what makes this a promising avenue is the potential for enterprising public-service providers to be unleashed from some of the restrictions of the public sector, yet driven by community purpose, asset locked and with greater levels of staff and community engagement. This opens up the possibility of managing the application of public money through appropriate governance at the highest level – aligning incentives between taxpayer, providers and service users – rather than through the minutiae of contractual legalese, thereby reducing complexity and costs.

Taken together, steps like this would represent an evolution towards a more co-operative state, in terms of the way it exploited the fiscal, regulatory and spending levers at its disposal. This would, in turn, prompt the development of a more co-operative private sector, itself working more in the common interest.

Problems with the social sector

So a co-operative model may offer an alternative to some of the failures of the public and private sectors. But, as Raymond Williams pointed out as early as 1962: 'We have been reduced to making contrasts between the speculator and the bureaucrat, and wondering which is the blacker devil. The real barrier, perhaps, is that we see these as the only alternatives'.[13]

So what about the sector that defines itself through its social, and supposedly more co-operative, ethos: civil society, the social sector or the voluntary and community sector? Whatever we call it and however we define it, and despite its positive net worth in comparison to its public and private cousins, the social sector too suffers from a number of flaws and failures.

First and foremost, the social sector relies to a massive degree on the other two sectors. Organizations that exist beyond the control of the state for a social purpose rather than private profit are hugely reliant on the benevolence of public grants or contracts and private hand-outs. While they are defined in theory by their independence of governance, their practical existence is characterized by financial and indeed other forms of dependence.

In contrast to communist regimes, liberal democracies pride themselves on the role of a strong civil society existing independently of the ruling state ideology. Civil society under communism, to the extent it would exist at all, would be regulated, funded and governed in a way that was dominated by the state apparatus. Civil-society groups would be a) restricted from political activities; b) significantly reliant on state funding; and c) not truly independent, with the state directly influencing decision making and governance. Yet, worryingly, we can also recognize each of these patterns in the relationship between civil society and the state in the UK today.

When it comes to regulation, many civil-society organizations are regulated by charitable law. Most thinktanks are charities, for example. Yet a charity cannot exist for a political purpose, which includes 'securing or opposing a change in the law, policy or decisions' and 'an organization will not be charitable if its purposes are political'. Yet organizations are incentivized by the state to adopt charitable status and thus fall under these rules through – as Dame Suzi Leather puts it – 'generous tax breaks and other advantages'.

On the funding side, the state is a dominant source of income for the social sector: the 2012 NCVO Almanac tells us that between a third and a half of the voluntary sector's income comes from statutory sources.[14] Much of the rest comes from private sources, from individual donations, businesses and customers, but relatively little from within the sector itself.

In terms of governance, the 2011 Panel on Independence of the Voluntary Sector reported that 'state appears to exercise undue influence over the governance of charities... in some cases there is a sole trustee who is a local government employee... pressure can be put on them to include a local authority representative on their Boards'.[15]

So, for civil society in the UK today, political activities are restricted, government funding is critical and the state can restrict the independent governance of the sector. As the Independence Panel concluded, there are 'real and present risks' to independence and 'indirect and sometimes direct pressure towards self-censorship, muting the voice of some in the sector'.

A second major failure of civil society is that in accepting, albeit often reluctantly, the pervasiveness of the market mentality, the sector is increasingly tending towards the methods and mindset of competition, yet with no corresponding benefit to society. The transaction costs of competing for funds are enormous. Funds administered by NatWest, for example, as well as the UK government's Social Action Fund, have seen hundreds of organizations competing for resources with only a tiny percentage (less than one per cent) ultimately attracting funding. It is hard to see who is benefiting from such competition and how beneficiaries couldn't fail to see some rewards if charities co-operated to a greater extent.

A deeper co-operation

So a case can be made that imagines a more co-operative economy, in the sense that each distinct sector adopts a more co-operative approach – with co-operative businesses taking a higher market share and organizations in the public and third sectors mutualizing or embodying more co-operative principles. Yet this is only a co-operative alternative to capitalism in a limited sense – simply more co-operative actors playing the capitalist game. As far as it goes, this is perhaps not so hard to imagine.

But from a more fundamental perspective, which may be as difficult to conceive as Žižek suggests, such changes could be a stepping stone to the transformation of the relationships not only *within* but *between* the sectors, and the creation of a system of production that could be defined as an alternative to capitalism – or co-operativism.

This co-operative alternative to 'actually existing capitalism' would recalibrate a co-operative dynamic between sectors rather than the current competitive and antagonistic tension. This means players within the system realizing through enlightened self-interest that they will each benefit from working more effectively together to create a more successful, balanced and mutually supporting democratic mixed economy.

The official figures tell us that the public and private sectors are less than worthless, while the voluntary sector and private households maintain a net value of many trillions of pounds.[3] Simplistically, this could be interpreted as meaning that we, both as individuals and in association, are collectively carrying the public and private institutions. Alternatively, it could be argued that private business and government have overreached themselves for our sake – trying to deliver us the financial returns we have come to expect as investors, and the public services we have come to expect as citizens.

Either way, these figures illustrate how the interrelation between sectors is important for the ongoing viability and sustainability of the UK's economy and society. Yet this dynamic between sectors is bafflingly ignored by economists and demands greater consideration, especially as our two sectoral giants are currently practically bankrupt, if not technically insolvent. There are very few serious attempts to understand how the three spheres of labour and capital interrelate within our economy.

We do have theories of market socialism, such as the Lange

model of Pareto efficiency;[16] studies of common resource management, led by Elinor Ostrom;[17] and Yochai Benkler's recent inquiry into how 'co-operation triumphs over greed'.[18] Indeed, Benkler does go some way towards exploring the relationship between different sectors of the economy, highlighting the extremes of Hobbes' Leviathan and Adam Smith's Invisible Hand.

But what do we really understand about the interrelationship between private individuals and businesses (competing to create financial wealth) with public bodies (which command or control resources to create public goods and services) and with the groups, charities, trusts and associations (which co-operate to make the country a more socially or environmentally rich place to live in)? In other words, what are the positive and negative economic dynamics between (crudely drawn) *liberté*, *egalité* and *fraternité*?

Can the state provide the infrastructure that helps businesses? Can businesses reinvigorate communities? Does the private sector generate tax revenues? Can social action save government money? Do markets rely on trust and social capital? And, more destructively, do businesses generate negative externalities which bring costs to the government? Does the public sector crowd out social action? Can the welfare system stifle enterprise?

Of course the answer is yes to all the above, to various degrees and dependent on the circumstances. A co-operative alternative to capitalism then, would see the pursuit of actions, policies and entrepreneurial approaches which lead to more positive supporting, catalyzing and enabling dynamics and less stifling, undermining and crowding out. The economy can be highly inefficient when these three different sectors work selfishly and destructively in opposition. The state is asked every year to pick up a bigger tab to solve the externalities and failures of the market, the private sector is feeding the public sector's addiction to tax revenues, and the social sphere is ever more reliant on hand-outs to shoulder the burden of mopping up failure elsewhere. Instead, a more harmonious and symbiotic alignment of the different spheres of capital and labour could lead to more sustainable public finances, more responsible business and to a more effective social sector.

This is related to what UK Labour Party leader Ed Miliband is driving at with his interest in 'pre-distribution', with the intention of reducing the need for fiscal transfers later – though this only considers the dynamic between the private sector and the state. It is also linked to the Conservative Party's 'Big Society' idea, with the argument that if the state gets out of the way, then social action can flourish – but this is only half of one side (and the gloomy side at that) of a triangle.

This is not a theory, then, which proposes market socialism from a negative position – as an alternative to the expropriation of surplus value by capitalists – but rather as a positive construction of a political economy that is more efficient *as well as* more social. Admittedly, there is currently little evidence that such a system would indeed be more efficient but, encouragingly, this is not because attempts have been tried and failed (and as a starting point, it seems we only need to improve upon a model running at 60-per-cent efficiency.)

Where there is some relevant evidence, perhaps, is in the natural world, where a range of research suggests that co-operation can be evolutionarily advantageous. The biologist Lynn Margulis, for example, has received much praise even from the supposed high prince of selfishness, Richard Dawkins, for examining how co-operation has been key to our evolution, arguing, for example, that 'life did not take over the globe by combat, but by networking.'[19] In *Evolution's Arrow*, John Stewart argued that 'evolution can exploit the advantages of co-operation by finding ways to make co-operation pay for the individuals who co-operate'.[20] Work by Robert Trivers on 'reciprocal altruism' suggested that helping another at your own cost in the short term may be beneficial in the long term and therefore evolve into a more permanent co-operative strategy.[21] Axelrod's *Evolution of*

Co-operation follows his work on the 'Prisoners Dilemma', which concluded that the most successful players were those who co-operated on the first move and then reciprocated what the other prisoner did on the previous move.[22] Similarly, Martin Nowak's *SuperCooperators* argues that 'co-operation, not competition, is the key to life' and that many of our great innovatory evolutions, from the molecular level to language and the city, have been driven through co-operation.[23] Bowles and Gintis' *Cooperative Species* also explores how co-operation has been crucial to human survival and progress.[24]

In contrast to the bibliography of inter-sectoral economics, the list goes on. But while we still await the emergence of a convincing new economics, these lessons from nature, together with recent evidence of the success of co-operatives on the ground, may be in themselves enough to suggest that the exploration of an economic system that more accurately reflects humanity, its motivations and behaviours, may be worthy of more serious consideration.

So is there a co-operative alternative to capitalism? Perhaps not, if what we mean by capitalism is a mixed market economy. But the answer is almost certainly yes, if we are in the market for an alternative to 'actually existing capitalism'. The recent history of the private, public and social sectors – and also the story deep inside us – could prompt a dawning realization by participants in the economy that a more co-operative approach could potentially deliver a more efficient, human and harmonious market economy in a world with ever scarcer resources. A co-operative economy can be in both our common and our self-interest. As Robert Owen says, 'the union and co-operation of *all* for the benefit of each.'[25] Imagine.

Dan Gregory is a policy adviser

1 Slavoj Žižek, *Living in the End Times*, Verso, London, 2010. 2 UK Treasury, Budget, 2012. 3 Office for National Statistics press release, 16 August 2012. 4 National Endowment for Science, Technology and the Arts, 'Atlantic Drift', 2011. 5 UK

Competition Commission, annual report and accounts, The Stationery Office, London, 2012. **6** S Bowles and H Gintis, *A cooperative species – human reciprocity and its evolution*, Princeton University Press, Princeton and Oxford, 2011. **7** *The Guardian*, 26 June 2011. **8** Social Enterprise Live, 11 July 2011, nin.tl/13TCepm **9** Social Enterprise UK, 'Fightback Britain', 2011, nin.tl/10pNRYB **10** C Bajo & B Roelants, *Capital and the Debt Trap*, Palgrave Macmillan, New York, 2011. **11** Plunkett Foundation, 'Community-owned village shops: A better form of business', 2011, nin.tl/13TCPr2 **12** See a number of *Third Sector* (thirdsector.co.uk) and *Building Design* (bdonline.co.uk) articles. **13** Raymond Williams, *Communications*, Penguin, 1962. **14** J Clarke, D Kane, K Wilding & P Bass, UK Civil Society Almanac 2012, National Council for Voluntary Organisations. **15** Panel on the Independence of the Voluntary Sector, 'Protecting Independence: the voluntary sector in 2012', nin.tl/10pOLEr **16** O Lange, 'On the Economic Theory of Socialism', *The Review of Economic Studies* V4, 1936. **17** E Ostrom, *Governing the Commons*, Cambridge University Press, 1990. **18** Y Benkler, *The Penguin and the Leviathan*, Random House, 2011. **19** L Margulis & D Sagan, *What is Life?*, Weidenfeld and Nicholson, London, 1996. **20** J Stewart, *Evolution's Arrow*, Chapman Press, Canberra, 2000. **21** R Trivers, 'The Evolution of Reciprocal Altruism', *Quarterly Review of Biology*, 46, 1, 1971. **22** R Axelrod, *The Evolution of Co-operation*, New York, 1984. **23** M Nowak, *SuperCooperators*. Free Press, New York, 2011. **24** S Bowles & H Gintis, *A Co-operative Species*, Princeton, 2011. **25** Robert Owen, *The Social System*, 1826.

5
Between the market and the state

Daniel Crowe

The co-operative alternative to capitalism exists. It is very real, very present and very practical. Every day, in numerous sectors of the economy and across a range of goods and services co-operative enterprise is in action, owned by and in return benefiting an estimated billion people across the world. Many members might not be conscious of it, and only a small minority might play an active, involved role in the governance of their co-operative, but collectively the power of co-operation is a formidable proposition with the potential to change the world.

Unlike capitalism, which at best has been an engine of technological advancement and rising living standards, and at worst an exploiter of labour, plunderer of resources and polluter of our biosphere, co-operation is more than an economic system, a business model or a simple way of meeting social and individual needs through the pursuit of self-interest. Co-operation is a profound and revelatory concept that offers a holistic approach and practical route to achieving fundamental social, economic and political objectives. With roots in the worlds of science and philosophy, co-operation exists both as an ideological underpinning for a new, democratized, political economy, and as a tangible, organizational response to the many challenges faced by our species, and our inadequate stewardship of our planet and its resources.

Whatever challenges humanity faces, co-operative endeavour and enterprise through the application of co-operative values, principles and organizations is proving to be a more economically equitable, environmentally sustainable and socially empowering solution than any capitalist construct or state intervention. To date, it is nation states, their governments and the untrammelled forces of capitalism that have mostly served to shape our world, bringing forth unimaginable riches and advancement, and also abject poverty and chaos. But it is co-operation which offers the greatest hope for our future development. If we shine a light, even in the most wretched and destitute corners of our world abandoned by the state and only exploited by capital, we can find the motivating spirit of mutual advancement that is co-operation.

For co-operation is not just capitalism's alternative – it is also the alternative to the state. Co-operation is a unique hybrid of interests, roles, remits and responsibilities that can make it so simple to grasp yet so complicated to explain. Co-operatives are market-facing entities, in competition not just with private enterprise and state companies, but also with other co-operative and mutual enterprises. To survive, they must be successful: making a return on capital employed, meeting member and wider customer needs, and making and successfully reinvesting profits. But co-operatives also share characteristics of the state: securing, stewarding and democratically controlling resources and capital for a collective membership, deploying it according to member priorities and a codified set of values and principles. And, to further complicate matters, co-operatives can lay a claim to a position straddling what Friedrich Hayek termed the 'third sector' between state and market.

That co-operation can be difficult to categorize and an

uncomfortable fit within a defined typology is due to its multi-faceted nature. Capitalism finds its structural rationale in the model of competition best popularized as Darwinist 'survival of the fittest', its performance measured in economic terms through boom and bust business cycles, its achievement of innovation and success via Schumpeter's process of 'creation through destruction', and its justification in classical economic theory through an appeal to self-interested utility maximizers. By contrast, co-operation can locate its scientific justification in evolutionary biological theories from Kropotkin's 'mutual aid' to the co-operation of genes elaborated upon by Dawkins, as well as validation across a range of political-science disciplines from game theory to behavioural economics. It is in its practice, however, that its relevance as an alternative to the current mainstream way we conduct business and organize society can be most clearly distinguished.

The many forms of capitalism

Before we look at what we mean by an alternative to capitalism, we must first understand what we mean by capitalism, the part it plays in our way of life as individuals and communities, its wider impact on society, and its crucial role in our national economy, our political system and in our increasingly globalized world. Much confusion and white noise distorts the debate around the current 'crisis of capitalism', the alleged failure of neoliberalism and free-market ideology that is lumped together with a condemnation of ownership structures responsible for wealth and power accruing to a tiny global élite, while inequality is increasingly rampant within nations as much as between continents.

We are now in the middle of a global financial crisis. This is blamed by some on the state (through the pursuance by central banks of an ultra-loose monetary policy and weak regulatory oversight of the banking industry) as much as on the unchecked animal spirits of financial capital that created increasingly complicated financial products, which in turn fuelled the long boom, property bubble and catastrophic collapse of the past decade. Against this backdrop, the co-operative alternative should be a shoo-in.

Unfortunately, for a number of reasons, it is not. While the number of people seeking solutions, answers and alternatives to the problems we face is growing, activism and the accompanying commentary is channelled into occupations and anti-market attitudes that provide no practical response. They can result in nihilistic anti-capitalism or to calls for greater public ownership through nationalization. And they can produce protests against states and governments, either for pursuing austerity or for taxing and spending, with the latter calling for greater privatization and shrinkage of the state.

Confusion surrounding this crisis, together with deep-seated ideological beliefs and political positioning, has paradoxically either led to calls for greater state intervention and a rolling-back of markets and or the contrary approach: a rolling back of the state and increase in supply-side reform to 'liberate' markets. Most of those on either side of this divide also call for a more responsible capitalism, which could be seen as oxymoronic without legislation to compel organizations to put wider issues or social and environmental concerns before profit maximization. Despite these contradictory prescriptions, in reality capitalism and state intervention are so intertwined that our current mixed economy is likely to be a reality for decades to come. It is, however, this space that provides the greatest opportunity for the co-operative alternative to grow.

The state's bailout of Long Term Capital Management in 1998 put paid to the myth of *laissez faire*, and the recent round of nationalizations and state intervention following the financial earthquakes caused by the decision to avoid moral hazard by letting Lehman Brothers collapse has again put the role of the state centre stage as the primary and pre-eminent alternative vehicle to capitalism. But such a position ignores the reality of markets, conflating capitalism with a market economy, and the state with liberal democracy. In reality, just as there are many kinds of state regime, there are many forms of capitalism.

We are familiar with our Anglo-Saxon model, predicated as it is towards shareholder value and short-term profit maximization against long-term investment, as well as private equity arrangements that encourage asset-stripping and greater returns on capital investments. We can counterpose these with continental models, such as Germany's evolving Rhineland model with its corporatist approach and greater involvement of workers and unions in strategic decision-making. And we also have the diversity of emerging models of capitalism as practised in the BRICS and beyond: from the oxymoronic state capitalism of China; the crony capitalism of illiberal Russia; the emerging capitalism of the South American leftist regimes; and the dictatorial capitalism of the Middle Eastern sovereign wealth funds.

These various models of capitalism have had a profound effect on our human condition, on society and the world we inhabit. Since industrialization, they have played a key role in the rapidly unfolding environmental catastrophe as much as helping to create a consumer culture. We could hold unbridled capitalism responsible for these and other consequences, and blame the markets for the inefficient allocation of capital, the ascendance of financial over manufacturing capital, the short-termism of shareholders and the casino mentality of players on the global financial markets.

However, it would be a mistake to blame markets for the features associated with the pre-eminent model of economic endeavour and enterprise – the limited company – just as it would be erroneous to blame the worst cases of state abuse of human rights on the very real human need to organize our affairs collectively, taxing populations and assets to pay for public goods that the market cannot supply.

It is more helpful to see the market as the playing field, the arena, the pitch upon which economic competition is played out, or as a theatre of enterprise, populated by billions of characters, each making choices over goods and services.

The state is the referee, the umpire, the rule-maker and the law-enforcer. Where the state is not active in a particular market, or in a market which is dominated by exploitative monopolies and rent-seekers, ordinary people have come together to create co-operative solutions to meet shared, local needs – from the folk of Rochdale in 1844 who so successfully codified co-operative enterprise, to the 20th-century pioneers who harnessed the power of globalized markets to promote a vision of fairly traded products.

Playing many parts

As human beings in this never-ending race to invent, innovate, produce, distribute, trade and consume, we are multi-role players. As citizens we exercise democratic choices in a political marketplace through the ballot box (and that increasingly rarefied activity, party political membership), which, while vitally important for choosing the umpires and setting the rules, currently seems to have increasingly little resonance in or direct relevance to people's lives.

As producers, unless we benefit from industrial democracy through an employee-owned organization, we may have little influence on our own activity, whether it is directed by a public bureaucracy to meet social ends or a commercial entity to meet private ends. And as consumers, we are limited in fulfilling our needs and meeting our desires through choices in the market only by our means to pay, but remain largely distant from any sense of ownership or influence over a product, service or organization that brings these to market, bar perhaps nostalgic affinity to a once-great British brand that is threatened with foreign ownership.

So our roles are never wholly complete – we remain largely divorced from each of these key areas of activity. Of course, it doesn't have to be this way. The key thread running through each of these areas – democratic ownership – is what constitutes the central core of co-operation. Where *bona fide* co-operatives are active, ownership and influence through democratic engagement by the membership is a central feature. And co-operatives bring this feature of democratic ownership and control to any number of markets or areas of human activity, recognizing that the best way to meet individual aims is through joining forces and resources through common endeavour, in our role as citizens, producers and consumers.

This vast economic stage is therefore also home to a younger challenger to both the traditional capitalist model and to state provision, often in the dark, often waiting in the wings, far removed from the spotlight. For to date, the co-operative has been the understudy to the principal actors, capital and the state, only performing where markets fail or do not seek to compete as it is deemed unprofitable, or when the state's top-down bureaucratic solutions are unsuitable and unsustainable.

The absurdity of our economic and political drama continues: bankrupt states are offering only austerity, while the residualized social democracies are promising more rehashed one-size-fits-all programmes and projects that continue to do things to people instead of seeking to empower, educate and resource them to do things for themselves; capitalist companies, meanwhile, are subject to increasing levels of distrust, alienation and cynicism as to their motives and the ethos of their operating model. In these circumstances, it is time for co-operation to assume centre stage. But as we step out and seek to upstage the powers of state and capital we need to make sure we know our lines.

We have to be open and honest and admit that, compared to the might of capitalism and the prerogative of the state, we might currently at best be marginal, but that we are the vanguard of a democratizing wave that will wash over our politics, our societies and our economies. We are a movement that seeks to put capital back into the hands and under the direction of the people, rather than defer responsibility to a remote bureaucracy, or leaving it to the profiteers with no allegiances other than Mammon.

We need to say no, this isn't a cuddly, wishy-washy, creed for liberal do-gooders or a synonym for state activity – this is a hands-on organizational model that is tough and robust, based on the notion that people and communities have to help themselves, that they shouldn't rely on the state to support them or keep allowing capitalist concerns to exploit them. We need to argue that instead of blaming, protesting, lamenting and criticizing, and relying on others to do things for us, we need to take action ourselves and get involved.

This is the alternative. No-one should expect things to be done for them: not by governments, not by private enterprise. This is our message: for too long people have withdrawn from meaningful political, economic and social life, expecting things to be delivered for them, with little thought behind how things are made, how their consumer choices are influencing wider economic and social outcomes, and how political processes are conducted, decisions are made and resources allocated.

This needs to change – and co-operation provides the vehicle to do so. People need to take democratic ownership and control of their own lives – choosing voluntarily to associate and act in solidarity, equity and equality to pool their power and resources and achieve more together than they can as individual citizens, producers and consumers. This is our business model – yes, it's tough, but it's also one that cares about other human beings, about the communities we live in and the world we inhabit.

It is a model and an ideology that seeks revolutionary social and economic change. It is this vision of a future co-operative society that so inspired the original architects, visionaries and pioneering practitioners of the movement. They, like us today, know that our values and principles are timeless, and are of benefit to all humanity. But they are no use as words on a page. They need to be heard and acted upon. If, as that great chronicler of the human condition, Shakespeare, once said, 'all the world's a stage', we need to get out there, pull no punches, and 'speak the speech' – or tell it like it is.

This is co-operation. There is no other alternative.

Daniel Crowe works on promoting co-operation at a local level.

6
Working towards economic democracy
James Doran

Introduction

Though individual workers may own capital – with deferred wages invested through pension funds, and ownership of potentially productive assets such as a house or apartment – housing is predominantly used for residence rather than as a source of rental income, and pension funds are not directly accountable to their members. So, even though they are in a majority, workers cannot be considered to be a ruling class, despite the prevalence of representative democracy within contemporary capitalism. Representative democracy is, moreover, currently limited to the state. Corporate boardrooms are the last rotten boroughs in existence: the governance of capitalist firms, from banks to the corporations they finance, does not proceed according to accepted notions of democratic representation. This has a damaging impact on the capacity of affected individuals to protect and pursue their interests as free and equal citizens.

Capitalism cannot be understood as merely a system in which markets function because both its predecessor, feudalism, and its 20th-century rival, state socialism, were societies with market exchange. Capitalism is an economic system characterized by large concentrations of wealth and power in plutocratic organizations that are autonomous. Corporations stand apart from the individuals they benefit, though they are recognized as corporate individuals by the state, acquiring the rights of real human beings. This gives their owners the privilege of limited liability without the responsibility of adopting a system of representative democracy in corporate governance.

Understanding capitalism in these terms has been made harder by the legacy of the Cold War, in which the rivals were portrayed as being engaged in a battle between capitalism and communism, which with the collapse of communist states in Europe has come to be understood as the discovery that capitalism is the best possible economic system, or perhaps the least bad. This has had an impact on how criticisms of economic reality under capitalism – and proposals for reforms – could be presented.[1] During the 1990s, writers like Will Hutton in Britain, and academics such as Margaret M Blair in the US, developed a critique of shareholder value maximization which could fit within existing discourses on market economies. A descriptive 'team production' approach, exploring the co-operative relationships within firms that contributed to success, was used to put forward a normative theory as to how reforms to corporate governance could produce 'stakeholder firms', and even a 'stakeholder society' – but one which could safely be described as capitalist.[2]

Today, capitalism is in crisis. In fact, capitalism is crisis, as there is a systemic need to find new outlets for profitable investments, new markets trading new commodities which will allow quantitative capital accumulation to continue – and so the system is unable to resolve global environmental problems of climate change and natural resource depletion, which involve non-capitalist forms of capital. And at the same time, there is a global financial crisis which has become a crisis of the state:

across the Western world, advanced capitalist states have bailed out the investor-owned financial services sector. As a consequence, governments are implementing harsh austerity cuts to public services, jobs and pensions, cutting social-security payments for the poorest to pay for a crisis caused by the richest. Employment protection is being weakened, making labour markets more 'flexible' for employers and more precarious for workers. Whereas previous periods of austerity appeared to be temporary, lasting a few years before a revival of economic growth allowed services and standards to be restored through struggle, the current crisis is presented as a necessary requirement: austerity for the many to allow continued prosperity for the few.

The global Occupy movement spread throughout the Western world in 2011 following the uprisings in the Middle East and North Africa against corrupt dictatorships and economic hardship. Just as Egyptian revolutionaries camped in Tahrir Square in Cairo to demand the fall of the dictatorship and to discuss the potential of political democracy, the Occupy camps in large cities across the West demanded reform of the bailed-out banks and discussed the link between economic power and democratic participation. Because of this, it became possible to use the word 'capitalism' to describe a split between the rich and the rest, 'the 1 per cent' ruling over 'the 99 per cent'. If nothing else was achieved, millions of ordinary people were able to understand that the economic hardship they were suffering was as a result of a systemic failing which would endure, rather than a personal failing or a temporary situation – this reality could not be denied by political élites, nor evaded by the ruling class.

Co-operativism

Is there, then, a desirable alternative to capitalism? This essay will argue that, yes, there is an alternative: co-operativism. As a political philosophy, co-operativism posits that the voluntary and autonomous association of individuals on the basis of equal, democratic and economic participation, will provide the material basis for the development of a critical consciousness and the establishment of links with other co-operatives, resulting in further co-operation. The history of past alternatives, their weaknesses, limitations and failures, would suggest that co-operativism – as a set of ethical values associated with the co-operative movement and as a vision of a future co-operative commonwealth – is a potential successor to a system of capitalist rule, given the right mix of conditions.

For co-operative enterprise to become the form of economic organization which predominates, agents of change will have to be identified and brought together by the co-operative movement. Other social movements will have to recognize the value of a systemic shift from capitalism and have a vision of how transformation will take place. This interaction currently occurs, but in an organic and nascent fashion which requires conscious political organization and structured political education.

The main ally in challenging the power of the capitalists' system will be that other great democratic movement – organized labour. It will be necessary for co-operative trade associations and the peak federations of trades unions to collaborate at national and transnational levels to develop and publicize models of co-operative enterprise. Both movements will have to view their future success as being directly dependent upon the other if co-operativism is to be established.

This is possible, and is already happening. To give one example, in the US the United Steelworkers Union (USW) has entered into a partnership with Mondragon International, the global arm of the world's biggest league of worker co-operatives).[3] Their aim is to establish new 'union co-ops' which the workers will own and the USW will organize as the trade union, collectively bargaining with management on pay and conditions and also helping workers to participate in the democratic processes of the co-operative. The motivation for the partnership is the bad experience that the USW had with employee share-ownership in capitalist firms, and the realization that co-operative ownership is more desirable; for the Mondragon co-operatives, it was felt that the firms that the group owned outside of Spain had to become co-operatives as well and to this end the USW could be of help.

But this essay does not refer to the numerous examples of where co-operatives and mutuals are already effectively practising 'non-capitalist' economics – building co-operativism within the shell of the existing capitalist economy – valuing workers, customers and local communities, while attempting environmentally sustainable development.[4] Rather, the emphasis here is on the theoretical basis for both the co-operative and trades union movements to advocate a systemic alternative.

Remembering membership

The distinction made by the socio-economist Johnston Birchall between investor-owned and member-owned businesses is key to understanding the future of progressive inclusion.[5] We are very familiar with enterprise as a means to provide a financial return to investor-owners, but we are much less familiar with member-owned businesses – there is a sense in which they are an exception to the rule. Co-operative and mutual enterprises offer a democratic alternative to the domination of investor interests, including excluded categories of people such as employers and consumers, and allowing other forms of wealth to be created.

If the corporation can be imagined as a republic of capital, then representative democracy needs to replace the limited franchise which currently exists: divorcing the voting power of the individual from the value of their equity stake will be crucial. But there is a concern amongst many contemporary co-operators that the movement would be seen as authoritarian if it were explicitly to argue that all organizations in society should function co-operatively. For example, in his excellent review of the role of co-operative enterprise in an age of capital, John Restakis argues against advocating the conversion of all enterprises into co-operatives on exactly these grounds.[6]

However, it would in fact be a matter of modifying the legislation concerning a privilege granted by the state to individuals, rather than a draconian imposition of enforced freedom at gunpoint. It would not be denying liberty, but extending it. If democratic governance were to be enshrined in company law, currently disenfranchised workers and consumers would be empowered by such a reform.

It was with the aim of reviving the democratic alternative to both centralized state socialism and free-market capitalism, and thus re-establishing a tradition overshadowed by the post-War consensus and actually existing socialist states, that Paul Hirst attempted to popularize a normative theory of associationalism.[7]

Hirst incorporated concepts developed by Albert O Hirschmann with regard to individual responses to organizational decline. The three options available are: exit, leaving the organization; voice, expressing their views on what is going wrong and what should be done to put it right; and loyalty, saying nothing and acting as if everything is fine.[8] Hirst wanted affected interests to have the ability to exit or express their voice through democratic processes, but what was missing from his core associationalist principles was any explicit mention of decommodification: in this case, the ending of ownership as a commodity which can be traded.[9]

In certain ways, Hirst's work on associational socialism was predated by the writings of Paul Derrick. Derrick was a Christian socialist and a co-operator; his remarkable book *Lost Property: Proposals for the Distribution of Property in an Industrial Age* was published in 1948 and reissued in the 1980s, but is currently out of print. Derrick's vision in this book mapped out a coherent alternative to capitalism, but his proposals were not taken up by anti-capitalists operating both in and outside the Labour Party in the post-War period. However, he continued to write on the subject of co-operativism until his death, arguing that to 'turn a capitalist economy into a socialist one is not to nationalize this company or that; it means incorporating the co-operative principles of a limited return on capital and democratic control in company law'.[10]

Democracy at work?

Michael Albert and Robin Hahnel have developed a vision of 'participatory economics' which owes much to the libertarian socialist tradition.[11] They propose that democratic firms should institute 'balanced job complexes': each employee's role combining mental and manual tasks, ensuring that all are able to participate in decision-making; there would be iterative planning processes between firms and a nested hierarchy of worker and consumer councils.

From a non-socialist liberal perspective, the economist David Ellerman has made a Lockean argument for democratic control of the firm by the workforce.[12] This normative 'labour theory of property' is based on a descriptive approach to the labour process: in a capitalist firm, wage-earners enter the workplace, 'mix their labour' with means of production to create added value, and leave the employer to dispose of this newly created property. The wage they are paid for this work does not typically reflect directly the revenue generated for the firm through the sale of the property, namely goods and services, that the workers have created. Ellerman argues that this can be resolved through democratic ownership, taking to the logical conclusion the claims of trades unions for collective bargaining and worker-participation through board-level representation.

From a Marxian perspective, Samuel Bowles and Herbert Gintis have echoed the arguments in favour of broad participation in corporate governance, and responded to the claim that democratic firms are inherently less efficient by describing the way in which capitalist firms are hindered by 'contested exchange' between labour and capital.[13] If labour is a cost to be minimized and capital has a claim which is to be maximized, then there is competition rather than co-operation between affected individuals.

The importance of 'tacit knowledge', a concept advanced by the neoliberal Hayek in defence of capitalism,[14] can be applied at the level of the firm as well as in society as a whole. The tacit knowledge possessed by workers in an enterprise is crucial to improving productivity, and where exchange is contested between capital and labour, this knowledge is unlikely to be made explicit so as to be put to good use in resolving problems and making improvements.[15] The legacy of the economic calculation debate in the 1930s and the experience of actually existing socialism has led many contemporary Marxists to advocate the model of co-operative enterprise.[16]

One claim against increasing the number of labour-managed firms is that there is, in fact, no injustice at work: in capitalist firms, each factor of production is rewarded for its contribution. This is the theory, prevalent in mainstream economics, which denies there is a trade-off, or an exploitative relationship, detrimental to the interests of labour. Just as the work of employees is rewarded by a wage, it is claimed, capitalists are rewarded with interest or a dividend in return for the use of their capital. However, if this were the case, the directors of firms would treat the payment for use of capital as a cost to be reduced – firms would seek to limit the return on capital. Workers demanding pay increases are asked to moderate their claims for the benefit of the firm – but no such claims are made where shareholders are concerned.

Another concern raised when moves in the direction of workplace democracy are proposed is that it is possible – indeed, under capitalism, probable – that workers will be tasked with better managing their own exploitation and this may result in a replication of the undemocratic workplaces of capitalist firms. This is why ownership matters as much as processes of democratic participation: without shared ownership, the effective politicization of corporate governance cannot take place, as the claims of external investors will take place over workers who are without an ownership stake in the firm.

It is also argued against an economy of labour-managed firms that the interests of customers will be compromised by the decision-making bias towards workers. If there is choice within product markets, a deterioration in the quality of goods could be prevented by the process of competition between labour-managed firms providing rival goods or services. But assuming that the purpose of the firm remains profit-maximizing, and does not focus upon ethical profit-making, then there is reason to expect the interests of existing customers could suffer. For example, more affluent customers could be prioritized over those existing customers who may be less affluent. This is why there is a great degree of scepticism in the trades union movement about the ability of co-operatives or mutuals to provide public services in the context of ongoing austerity programmes and the possibility of co-payment replacing the model of universal service provision – the risk is that workers will be forced to prioritize those with the ability to pay over people with needs but without the means of paying for services.

A post-neoliberal era?

There are strong grounds in evidence for opposing the investor-owned model: during the global recession which began in 2008, few co-operative banks, building societies or credit unions required state bail-outs – unlike the many investor-owned financial firms which were in need of extraordinary assistance; perhaps for this reason, deposits in building societies and credit unions have increased.[17] And research suggests that employee-owned businesses have had a competitive advantage over other firms during the recession; it can be argued that the higher level of trust and motivation generated by the model of ownership creates more resilient businesses.[18]

But what's remarkable about the current crisis is not the endurance of neoliberal ideas and policies, but that social democracy cannot explain why this is the case. Social democratic politicians in western Europe have become fond of using the slogan 'a market economy, not a market society' in an attempt to draw a veil over the reality of capitalist accumulation, suggesting to party activists and radical voters that the process of commodification can be contained within existing marketplaces.

There is hope in the adoption of Jakob Hacker's concept of 'predistribution' by Ed Miliband, the leader of the British Labour Party, to explain the redistribution of power within a market economy which could lead to a more equitable distribution of wealth and income.[19] It has signalled to journalists and commentators that measures can be taken by legislators which are qualitative, relational, and which do not necessarily involve large-scale redistribution as commonly understood to mean either taxation or nationalization. The message to the electorate is obviously much simpler, with talk of restoring the 'British Promise' that the next generation will have a better life than the last – in the context of a double-dip recession and harsh austerity measures, this is a cautiously optimistic offer.[20] The predistribution agenda echoes the ideas of the liberal-socialist philosopher John Rawls on property-owning democracy as a condition for justice, and it is not one that can be pursued without making enemies in powerful places.[21] Changes to corporate governance, competition policy and financial regulation are carefully posed in the context of a more 'responsible capitalism', however.

Entering a truly post-neoliberal era will require governments with the political will, alliances between the trades union and co-operative movements, and a much wider understanding of capitalism than currently exists amongst ordinary people.

Re-embedding markets, not (just) re-regulation

In previous economic systems, accumulation was strictly regulated. In the feudal era which preceded capitalism, for example, usury – lending money at interest – was tightly restricted by statutes and customs. Capitalist accumulation required that existing boundaries, ethical as much as spatial, were overcome – enabling new markets to be created for the profitable investment of surplus capital in the production and exchange of new commodities.[22]

Market forces as advocated in neoliberal theory, and described by Karl Polanyi, are a world away from a free and competitive market understood as an equal number of buyers and sellers; in *The Great Transformation*, Polanyi described the 'double movement' which occurred when the state acted to expand markets and then when the public responded to this change – this is symptomatic of the capitalist system.[23] The championing of market forces amounts to a defence of monopoly power, that of the capital-owner over other members of the capitalist firm, and that of capitalist firms over democratically elected governments that fail to implement sufficient pro-capitalist policies.

As the philosopher Slavoj Žižek points out, when the conditions that constitute market failure are examined in relation to the capitalist firm, it is clear that it violates the ideal market rules on all counts: in terms of scarcity of power, the capitalist enjoys an *a priori* structural advantage; in relation to information, the capitalist's access is *a priori* more complete, since s/he organizes the whole process and as far as externalities are concerned, the capitalist can ignore them, while the worker *is* (as a person who is not *only* a worker) in her/himself the affected externality.[24]

In this sense, capitalism is actually 'the zone of the anti-market', because crucial decision-making takes place outside of the marketplace, within hierarchical structures.[25]

The process of capitalist accumulation results in a capital glut, a surfeit of capital which necessitates expansion into new markets and the creation of new commodities.[26] This is apparent when the origins of the shadow banking system are considered: what is it that motivated the explosion in financial derivatives? It was precisely efforts to resolve the 'capital surplus absorption problem'.[22]

It is certain that on a finite planet, ever-increasing trade cannot continue: the unequal exchange of natural resources, known as 'environmental load displacement', is a process which threatens the biodiversity of ecosystems and the sectoral mix of economies in both the domestic and export markets.[27] 'Free' trade and 'free' markets have costs – the need of capital for continuing accumulation threatens the stability of communities when goods and services which could be produced or provided by local labour are instead imported.[28]

A model of prosperity without growth in throughput of natural resources, as proposed by Tim Jackson,[29] is certainly required. But a stationary or steady-state economy most obviously conflicts with the interests of capital-owners – a fossil oligarchy of corporations and financial institutions with substantial investments in carbon-based energy sources which have yet to be realized.[30]

Even without challenging the power of the capitalist class on environmental grounds, as Aaron Peters points out,[31] there are tendencies at work that make growth rates impossible to recover – in particular, what Marx called the 'moral depreciation' of machines, the inability to realize the surplus value of fixed capital when new and more profitable versions of existing machines are introduced. This destruction of value is apparent even in sunset industries such as information technology, making a new information capitalism unlikely to bear sufficient fruit.

To conclude this section on re-embedding markets within democratically determined processes, it is worth making explicit some important distinctions. With regard to alternative models to capitalism, the economist Pat Devine reminds us that 'the continued existence of labour markets, in which people agree to participate in production in exchange for income, and of consumer markets, in which consumer goods and services are bought and sold, is not at issue'.[32]

Devine emphasizes an important difference between the concept of 'market exchange', which describes the act of buying and selling, and that of 'market forces', which specifically refers to the drives that motivate interactions – and, as a result of competition in a capitalist market between profit-maximizing firms, these are short-term considerations which can overlook the value of certain inputs.

The economist Diane Elson has argued in favour of 'socialized markets' which would allow exchange to take place without subordinating economic activity to the power of a minority of capital-owners – the purpose of market regulation would thus be to re-embed markets within a democratic society.[33]

Another vital distinction has been made by William Davies in emphasizing the different dynamics arising as a result of the profit-*making* aim of co-operatives and mutuals, in contrast to the profit-*maximizing* aim of capitalist firms seeking to deliver shareholder value maximization.[34] Values such as patience, the concern for long-term commitment to a purpose, and well-being, the concern for happiness and democratic engagement, can be better realized through employee-owned firms that seek to make a profit, but not to maximize it by abandoning the purpose of doing business.[35]

Using 'commons' sense

How then can non-capitalist forms of value – social capital (relationships based on trust), human capital (the knowledge and skills people possess), and natural capital (the mineral resources and ecosystem services in existence) – be conceptualized without drawing equivalences with capitalist accumulation? The aim here is to avoid what JK Gibson-Graham referred to as 'capitalocentrism', the subordination of other forms of economic activity to the logic of capitalist accumulation.[4] Instead, language could be used which stresses common ownership and constructs a post-capitalist, 'commons' sense.

Commons are resources pooled between members of a community for either practical or ethical reasons. Land, forests, rivers and seas are all examples of possible common-pool resources. Constitutional or statutory protection of commons have been established in some states, and where commons are maintained they offer us an example of how, contrary to neoliberal theory, resources can be sustained by structures which are autonomous, beyond the direct control of either state or corporate bureaucracies.[36]

The re-commodification of healthcare, education and welfare systems in the advanced capitalist states could be resisted by demanding constitutional rights to these social commons: opposition to marketization and privatization should be reframed as opposition to the enclosure of these commons. It is in this spirit that the co-operative movement and the trades union movement should flow together – co-operating with other organizations in the movement to secure access to and development of the commons.

The provision of money, the means of exchange, is currently largely privatized, with capitalist financial institutions issuing much of the money supply.[37] Local currencies, managed by co-operatives, could stimulate and promote economic activity within towns and cities; in this way, whatever the future of the monetary system of the state, a monetary commons could flourish.[38]

Concern has been expressed – notably by the radical geographer David Harvey – that conceptualizing economic activity in terms of the commons could serve the systemic need of capitalism to have small-scale autonomous and thus competing organizations.[39] The divide between the public realm of municipalities and states and that of the commons has been addressed by Nick Dyer-Witheford in his categorization of the 'planner commons'.[40]

A non-capitalist and thus potentially post-capitalist 'circulation of the common' involves the planning and facilitation of 'commoning' through 'associations', such as the 'labour commons' of worker co-operatives – and with the aid of the state where there are supportive government initiatives – to produce yet more common-pool resources.[41]

Short of legislative change to democratize firms across the economy, it will be important for the co-operative and trades union movement to co-operate in assisting the mutualization of firms through employee trusts, buy-outs of firms experiencing succession failure, and the recuperation of abandoned plant and machinery by redundant workers.[42]

Worker co-operatives have tended to degenerate in isolation: if retired members are able to trade their ownership stake, if there is a fall in demand for the firm's products, or if there is an inability to adjust to technological change. Successful worker co-ops are often those which form part of a league – a co-operative of co-operatives that will guarantee workers a job in another firm if one enterprise ceases trading, that will offer training in response to technological change, or will help workers move into different roles. The endurance of the Mondragon co-operatives has depended upon this arrangement – and it is worth attempting to replicate the model of integrated financial services through a workers' bank, and research and development in co-operative educational institutions.

The formation of co-operative leagues has always been a political act – an attempt by ordinary people to control their working lives rather than be controlled by capital. How then to develop and communicate alternatives, to open up the media to new ideas and new areas of interest?

Education for co-operation is also key: within academia, there is the potential of broadening the curriculum in disciplines of economics and business management to examine the theory and practice of non-capitalist enterprise. And were the goal of co-operativism to be adopted by the trades union movement, it would be necessary to incorporate the study of co-operative and mutual enterprise in the training of trades union staff and the political education of lay activists.

Dan Hind has proposed media reforms which would allow common concerns to arise and enable the mass of people to become an engaged public.[43] Recognizing that, though politicians are accountable to citizens at election time, they prefer to monopolize what is considered political, and also cognizant of the biases that media ownership imposes on commissioners of investigative journalism, Hind proposes a system of 'public commissioning' which would give electors a vote on where to allocate a percentage of the public-service broadcasting budget. Associations of journalists, organized in worker co-operatives, would compete to offer investigative projects of interest to electors; the successful associations would then receive funding to carry out their work, contributing to the common knowledge of the public.

Hind has a broader agenda than media reform: he advocates public control of credit, wresting the power to create money from the private banking system, and he favours the democratization of the firm through restricting limited liability to companies which are employee-owned and democratically run. The assumption is that media reform would allow the formation of a public better able to strive for democratization of the economy as a whole.

Conclusion

The indirect way that this essay has dealt with its central argument – which is that the co-operative and trades union movements must unite towards the goal of co-operativism – is not an oversight, but a deliberate strategy. By way of conclusion, it is necessary to explain the rationale for an emphasis on the theoretical content rather than on the practical form that this alliance could take.

Approaching the subject of capitalism, of the role of trades unions and co-operatives in creating a new economic system, *without* being dismissed out of hand has been difficult for a long time. (I am intellectually indebted to Steve Akehurst, Éoin Clarke, Chris Cook, Dan Hind, Kieron Merret, Tom Miller, Richard Murphy, Aaron Peters, Ann Pettifor, Tom Powdrill, Carl Rowlands, Duncan Weldon, Adam White, and particularly to Martin Wood. But don't hold it against them.)

In the wake of neoliberalism's failed attempt to assert a hegemony of ideas, most working people now tend to have a depressive consciousness when it comes to progressive change, as the weight of debt and falling living standards holds down aspirations. This is why neoliberals are apt to point out that there's no appetite for an alternative – it's hard to imagine a future for humanity when there are so many other worries.

Social movements are not immune from these pressures: the growth and capacity of the Occupy movement, which arose in 2011, was inhibited by the fact that its members were ordinary working people, not all of them able to participate for long periods of time because of work commitments.

It is apparent that a lot remains to be worked through: the differences in understanding and approach within both the co-operative and trades union movements and the political parties which have the power to implement legislation enabling further co-operation to occur. But now that the idea of an alternative to capitalism is one that can no longer be dismissed, progress can be made towards a co-operative commonwealth.

James Doran is active within the British labour movement.

1 M Fisher, *Capitalist Realism: Is There No Alternative?*, Zero Books, 2009. **2** W Hutton, *The State We're In*, Jonathan Cape, 1995; MM Blair, 'Rethinking assumptions behind corporate governance', *Challenge*, Nov-Dec 1995. **3** C Davidson, '*Steelworkers Announce "Union Model for Bringing Worker-Owned Coops to the US*', 2010, nin. tl/12SsT64 **4** JK Gibson-Graham, *A Post-capitalist Politics*, University of Minnesota Press, 2006. **5** J Birchall, *People-Centred Businesses: Co-operatives, Mutuals and the Idea of Membership*, Palgrave Macmillan, 2011. **6** J Restakis, *Humanizing the Economy: Co-operatives in the Age of Capital*, New Society, 2010. **7** PQ Hirst, *The Pluralist Theory of the State*, Routledge, 1989. **8** AO Hirschmann, *Exit, Voice, and Loyalty*, Harvard University Press, 1970. **9** PQ Hirst, 'Renewing Democracy through Associations', *The Political Quarterly*, 73:4, 2002, pp 409-421. **10** P Derrick, 'Incomes Policy and Class Power', in *International Socialism* (1st series) Summer, 1966, pp 20-22. **11** M Albert & R Hahnel, *The Political Economy of Participatory Economics*, Princeton University Press, 1991. **12** DP Ellerman, *Property & Contract in Economics*, Blackwell, 1992. **13** S Bowles & H Gintis, 'A Political and Economic Case for the Democratic Enterprise', *Economics and Philosophy*, 9, 1993, pp 75-100. **14** FA Hayek, 'The use of knowledge in society', *American Economic*

Review, vol 35, 1945, pp 519-530. **15** F Adaman & P Devine, 'Socialist Renewal: Lessons from the "Calculation" Debate', *Studies in Political Economy*, 43, Spring, 1994. **16** MA Lebowitz, *Build It Now*, Monthly Review Press, 2006 ; H Shutt, *Beyond the Profits System*, Zed Books, 2010; RD Wolff, *Capitalism Hits the Fan*, Olive Branch Press, 2010. **17** J Birchall, & LH Ketilson, *Resilience of the co-operative business model in times of crisis*, ILO, 2009. **18** J Lampel, A Bhalla & P Jha, *Model Growth*, 2010, nin. tl/12Surx4 **19** J Hacker & P Pierson, *Winner-Take-All Politics*, Simon & Schuster 2010. **20** E Miliband, 'The Cost of Living Crisis Facing Britain', speech to the Resolution Foundation, 28 Feb 2011. **21** M O'Neill, 'Predistribution: an unsnappy name for an inspiring idea', *The Guardian* website, 12 Sep 2012. **22** D Harvey, *The Enigma of Capital and the Crises of Capitalism*, Oxford University Press, 2010. **23** K Polanyi, *The Great Transformation*, Beacon, 1944. **24** S Žižek, *Living in the End Times*, Verso, 2011. **25** F Braudel, *Civilization and Capitalism: 15th-18th Century* – Vol 2, Harper & Row, 1982. **26** H Shutt, *The Decline of Capitalism*, Zed Books, 2005. **27** A Hornborg, 'Zero-Sum World', *International Journal of Comparative Sociology*, Vol 50 (3-4), 2009, pp 237-262. **28** C Hines, *Localization – A Global Manifesto*, Earthscan, 2000. **29** T Jackson, *Prosperity Without Growth*, Earthscan, 2009. **30** E Altvater, 'The social and natural environment of fossil capitalism', in *Socialist Register*, 2007; *Coming To Terms With Nature*, ed L Pantich & C Leys, The Merlin Press, 2006. **31** A Peters, 'Forget the "golden age" of capitalism', in *Our Kingdom*, 6 Mar 2012, opendemocracy.net **32** P Devine, *Democracy and Economic Planning*, Polity Press, 1988. **33** D Elson, 'Socialized Markets, Not Market Socialism', *Socialist Register*, ed L Panitch & C Leys, Merlin, 1999. **34** W Davies, *Re-inventing the Firm*, Demos, 2005. **35** W Davies, *All of Our Business*, Employee Ownership Association, 2011. **36** E Ostrom, *Governing the Commons*, Cambridge University Press, 1990. **37** R Ryan-Collins, T Greenham, R Werner & A Jackson, *Where Does Money Come From?* New Economics Foundation, 2011. **38** M Mellor, *The Future of Money*, Pluto Press, 2011. **39** D Harvey, *Rebel* Cities, Verso, 2012. **40** N Dyer-Witheford, 'The circulation of the common', paper posted to *Species-Beings* blog, 30 Nov 2009. **41** Ibid; G de Peuter & N Dyer-Witheford, 'Commons and Co-operatives', *Affinities*, Vol 4, No 1, 2010, pp 30-56. **42** A Jensen, *Insolvency, Employee Rights & Buyouts*, Common Cause Foundation, 2005. **43** D Hind, *The Return of the Public*, Verso, 2010.

Co-operatives, open source and new global networks

7
Open source capitalism
Nic Wistreich

The response to the banking collapse – rescued by governments they had long bullied, and bailed out by the masses facing austerity, inflation and stagnant lending – has been somewhat muted. The Occupy movement revealed the scale of anger and illustrated the media-friendly potential of a mobilized and networked group, but often struggled to present a coherent alternative, split between reformists and revolutionaries, socialists and libertarians, the homeless and educated idealists.

If there was ever a time for the co-op movement to step forward with an alternative, it's now. Yet the world is very different from the one in which co-ops first emerged. Since before what some have called the early death-throes of neoliberalism, a different order has been emerging, far from the co-op space. The values of the Rochdale Pioneers live on, but are most widely visible and active today in the networked world. Non-capitalist, collaborative forces not only thrive in the networked world, but also provide much of its infrastructure. From gaming to the maker culture, people are motivated by forces other than profit, while some of the most commercially successful web businesses have been built upon Marxist ideas of getting the means of financing, production and distribution into the hands of everyone.

The web, as the biggest experiment in decentralized global collaboration in history, has been driven forward by two principles – open source software and motivation via social rather than monetary capital – which have more in common with co-operative values than with the free market. Noreena Hertz recognized in her essay for Co-operatives UK[1] that co-ops are the 'open source version of capitalism'. For those coming from open source software development, it could also be said that *open source is the co-op version of capitalism.*

For open source communities, the legal status of the entity co-ordinating large global collaborations seems less important to success than the style of management and methodology used, and co-ops are rare. But while there are many thousands of open source products which may not need a legal structure to create or distribute them, there are not yet many open source services which would depend on more complex corporate structures.

While co-ops and open source both exist within capitalism, they run contrary to its orthodoxy and could offer each other much: making the web more publicly controlled, and mobilizing networked people to solve complex real world problems. Utilizing motivators of human labour and innovation that are more powerful than the profit motive, and understanding how open source management empowers large decentralized collaborations to deliver solutions to problems, could be the key for co-operatives to not just flourish in the 21st century, but to address and solve many of the complex, interdependent problems facing the world.

The web is driven by non-market, co-operative forces

'Sometimes... non-market collaborations can be better at motivating effort and can allow creative people to work on

information projects more efficiently than would traditional market mechanisms and corporations. The result is a flourishing non-market sector of information, knowledge and cultural production, based in the networked environment, and applied to anything that the many individuals connected to it can imagine.'
Yochai Benkler, *The Wealth of Networks*[2]

Imagine an episode of the investment TV show *Dragons' Den* a decade ago. The budding entrepreneur begins to speak.

'I want to make a publication where millions of the biggest creators, brains and celebrities in the world, the leading filmmakers, artists, novelists, comedians, musicians, academics, technologists, journalists and business leaders will announce all their new work and ideas first. Many of them will provide a running commentary of their lives and work with photos, stories and videos – while they chat with each other and the rest of us.'

The incredulous dragons look on: 'Well, it sounds lovely, but how will you afford to pay them?' 'Oh, we won't... they'll do it for free.'

They would have been laughed out of the room, yet Twitter's ability to motivate, without cash, billions of hours of labour investment from highly skilled individuals doesn't seem strange, showing just how much the world has changed since the web exploded.

Nor is it unusual to any web native that much online activity appears to exist outside of market forces, with hundreds of millions of blogs, photos, videos and pieces of software created and shared for free and whose creators – more often than not – are not expecting a financial return, and certainly weren't motivated by that to create them. On Flickr, over 200 million photos have been tagged with Creative Commons licences allowing people to re-use those photos – often in commercial contexts – for free, in exchange for only a credit.[3]

It could be counter-argued that humans have been creating altruistically – or at least for reputational peer-status – for far longer than the web's existence (be it playing in a band, running a fanzine or painting watercolours) and that the web-based activities are nothing new, just more prominent due to network effects. But it isn't only personal creations that are being given away online – it's huge collaborative works.

The most famous is perhaps Wikipedia, with 23 million articles in 285 languages, 100,000 volunteer contributors and over 450 million unique monthly visitors.[4] We might again imagine the pitch in *Dragons' Den* – for an encyclopaedia bigger than Britannica which anyone could edit – being met with hysterics.

Less visible than Wikipedia but of wider impact, collaborative non-profit systems make up most of the architecture that powers the web and the digital economy. Tim Berners Lee's decision to release HTML into the public domain is considered to be one of the key factors in the web's success after similar proprietary systems emerged and failed in the preceding decades. Today anyone can contribute to and comment on discussion about the development of HTML through the Worldwide Web Consortium. Open source software, which broadly means software that can be freely shared, edited and rewritten (though it is not necessarily free) powers much more. There is the Linux operating system on which most servers run; the Apache server system which hosts the majority of websites;[5] the Android mobile operating system (built on Linux) which powers more smartphones than the iPhone; the majority of web browsers – from the Mozilla engine behind Firefox to the WebKit engine behind Safari and Chrome;[6] the overwhelming majority of content management systems such as Wordpress, Drupal, Joomla and hundreds more;[7] most coding languages – PHP, which powers Facebook and Wikipedia, Python, which runs Google and YouTube, and Ruby, which drives Twitter and Hulu.[8]

This isn't for lack of commercial competitors – Microsoft and other giants have battled to gain market share, spending tens of billions on proprietary browsers, servers, tools and languages – yet have mostly lost out to software that is open, free and normally created and driven by volunteers who have never met each other, collaborating from their computers around the world.

In 2010, $2.3 trillion worth of trade in the G20 alone was dependent on systems and software built and maintained outside of the capitalist concept of competition and financial incentive as the best driver of innovation and productivity. 'If it were a national economy, the internet economy would rank in the world's top five, behind only the US, China, Japan and India.'[9]

So what's driving this activity? Economic orthodoxy, right back to Adam Smith, is that the market and profit is the best motivator of human invention and productivity. What happened?

In his book *Drive*, Daniel Pink points to a major MIT study from 1969 that found money motivated people only up to a certain level.[10] Beyond this, performance deteriorated, regardless of the poverty or nationality of those being tested. The conclusion was that once people have their basic human needs covered – food, shelter, the ability to provide for their family and so on – money was no longer an incentive for better work, and, indeed, the more money that was at stake, the worse decisions people made. 'The best use of money as a motivator, is to pay people enough to take the issue of money off the table so that they are not thinking about money, but they are thinking about work,' he says.

Pink describes three key factors that motivate people once basic financial needs are addressed and which lead to both better performance and personal satisfaction:

autonomy – our desire to be self-directed, shaping our own lives

mastery – our urge to get better at something

purpose – our desire to work on something with meaning, values or a greater impact.

From Wikipedia to the open source movement, people have autonomous roles, and the chance to become better at something – be it their knowledge of a subject or their coding skills. There is also a strong purpose – to help educate the world or provide useful software for people who can't afford it. As Pink points out, the people who volunteer for these projects, often up to 20-30 hours a week, are mostly highly skilled and in-demand individuals with jobs.

Of course, this activity is from a mostly educated minority of the population – can similar non-market motivators be seen in the wider population? An obvious space would be the three billion human hours spent each week playing video games – an activity with huge autonomy and mastery, alongside a clear purpose – that, for the period of playing the game at least, is normally to defeat 'evil' or solve problems.

In her book *Reality is broken: why games make us better and can change the world*,[11] video games designer and activist Jane McGonigal argued that gaming contributed positively to human motivation and development, suggesting that we should play more games so as better to solve the problems of the world. Games are able to use fun in a way to create the right head-space needed to solve problems – readiness to collaborate, ingenuity and lateral thinking, confidence that success is possible, mastery and a refusal to be defeated despite regular failure.[12] She pointed out that the average young person in a country with a young gamer culture will have spent 10,000 hours by the time they are 21 playing games – the same amount of time, roughly, as they have spent in secondary school, and much of that time has involved learning, problem solving and often collaboration.

Games don't pay cash rewards but they do incentivize human labour, and many contemporary websites see 'gamification' – the use of video game-like rewards and ranks in web services and social networks – as the best way to build their popularity. The red buttons on Facebook saying how many new friends, messages or activities have recently occurred, or the number at the top of

Twitter explaining how many followers you have – all tap into a similar part of the psyche as a score in a video game and, indeed, they are usually placed in a similar part of the screen.

Where are the co-ops online?

'We need real open alternatives to cloud apps like Facebook. I don't mean hosted open source. I don't mean a better WordPress. I don't quite know what I mean, but I know I don't mean Zurker. I think the future has yet to be invented.'

Daniel Packer[13]

For all its open and collaborative foundations, the web has a monopoly problem. Facebook with social, eBay with auctions, Amazon with shopping, Twitter with micro-blogging, Paypal for payments, YouTube with video, Google with search, Apple with music, and so on – the market leader is typically one company, in a system where the biggest tend to get bigger.

While these companies produce some wonderful world-changing things, monopoly positions are clearly dangerous, making it easy to distort prices, censor, manipulate or flatten innovators. Amazon, for instance, charges publishers 65 per cent of the cover price to sell Kindle books over £8 ($13), nearly double the commission they took on physical books, and do that because they are in end-to-end control of their market. YouTube has been known to downgrade in search results videos that don't include their adverts. Apple's App Store has frequently run into trouble for censoring software they didn't like, such as one that reported on casualties from drone attacks.[14]

And while Facebook might be full of people sharing, writing and discussing for motives other than cash, and the service itself might use PHP and have open source software powering it, their management's legal obligation is to make a profit for their shareholders. Private equity and venture capital allowed them to scale up as quickly as needed in order to keep outgrowing the competition – but only under the expectation that they can turn the private and personal experiences of nearly a billion people into a commodity for targeted advertising. As the saying goes, you have the right to remain silent on Facebook, but anything you do say may be taken down and used in advertising against you.

You can imagine Alexander Graham Bell pitching the telephone to *Dragons' Den* under a similar business model... 'We'll be making this telephone free for everyone. And to pay for that we'll listen to your phone-calls and interrupt them with related adverts. We'll record them forever in a mostly public place, while the information we collect we'll share with companies and any government who asks.' Even the Dragons might have balked.

Since Facebook's rise to dominance there have been a number of attempts at more open alternatives. Even before it launched there were open source social networks people could host themselves, and services like Ning that let you host your own. In 2010 a group of NYC coders raised $200,000 from crowd-funding site Kickstarter to create a distributed social network that could (in principle) allow thousands of different websites – from newspapers and blogs to shopping and industry sites – to each host a bit of a bigger social network that would connect all of them. The source code is open, but in August 2012 the Diaspora founders handed over control to the community (leaving the future in question, with no legal entity or management structure fully responsible for it).

Tech entrepreneur Nick Oba attempted to launch a co-operative-owned social network, Zurker, and got a lot of blogosphere interest at the time of the Facebook IPO in mid-2012. Zurker offered members shares on signing up and referring friends so they could own a part of the site and share in its success. He received widespread coverage but ran into problems, with a user-interface far behind Facebook's, while he seemed to underestimate the unique conditions that supported

Facebook's success (like Twitter and YouTube, Facebook quickly managed to saturate a small, relevant market to the point where everyone 'had to have it' – in this case Harvard). Oba himself was frustrated at the management challenges of member voting:

'I'd say the biggest [challenge] is developing a system which allows democracy to function without degenerating into anarchy. A lot of folks equate member-driven democracy with a simplistic voting system – post a bunch of ideas, vote them up or down. But democracy is much more complicated than that, and any solution will have to be an ultra-sophisticated and carefully designed organism.'[15]

Most people's understanding of technical process is limited and open to their easily misunderstanding the trade-off between design, user interface, database architecture and code in building sites, given that most of this is hidden from view. One-member one-vote over key decisions in such a service could mean that experts are ignored and bad decisions made.

Zurker is currently offline and development seems to have stopped – which is not uncommon given how many new web start-ups come and go. What is most interesting is the level of publicity the service received once the idea was first widely discussed, with dozens of articles and bloggers wanting to support such a co-op, in spite of criticisms. A writer for *Wired* magazine said they found the proposition 'compelling, disruptive even. Zurker appeared to be flipping the status quo on its head. I enjoyed the notion of being rewarded for investment in time and engagement' though ultimately advising readers to 'be wary' of the site.[16]

A YouTube owned by filmmakers and cinemas could be just as popular and exciting as an Amazon owned by authors and independent bookshops – but in both cases success would only occur if the new services could match functionality and stability, with an easy way for people to migrate and a strong reason to do so beyond the virtuous (in other words, unique functions or features).

Another approach would be to educate and promote the benefits of switching to a co-op for existing web services, while encouraging new start-ups to consider taking that approach, and to make it easier (and clearly beneficial) to do so.

A breakthrough in managing large collaborations

'While *cheap internet was a necessary condition for the Linux model to evolve, I think it was not by itself a sufficient condition. Another vital factor was the development of a leadership style and set of co-operative customs that could allow developers to attract co-developers and get maximum leverage out of the medium.*

'*But what is this leadership style and what are these customs? They cannot be based on power relationships – and even if they could be, leadership by coercion would not produce the results we see.*'

Eric S Raymond, *The Cathedral & The Bazaar*[17]

There's much that can be said about the open source movement, and most people outside of the tech world seem to stop at the idea that 'it's free'. Except it often isn't, as Richard Stallman, who initiated the free software movement in 1983 is regularly at pains to express – free lunch or beer is different from free speech.[18] The freedom at its heart is the ability to see the code and make sure it isn't doing anything unsafe or unwanted, to edit and change it if you need to and to copy it as you need. If applied to hardware, a DVD player would be easily upgradable into a Blu-ray by the owner, or the iPhone 4 innards swiftly swapped for the iPhone 5 (or an Android), leaving the case intact.

But in the context of co-operatives, what is most promising about open source is the methods by which vast global, largely decentralized groups of people – who are mostly unpaid volunteers – collaborate to create complex solutions to quite specific problems, that frequently don't just equal, but surpass proprietary alternatives. That some of these solutions become billion-dollar profit-making companies like RedHat, some commercial free services like Wordpress, and others non-profit cash-rich giants like Mozilla, is perhaps secondary to the means by which open source projects bring about these solutions.

The world is clearly full of problems that require vast numbers of people collaborating and sharing knowledge across countries and education levels to solve them, and where there are often scarce resources to support that. Without addressing the management process first, the idea of adding collective ownership and democratic control over decisions would appear to be creating a further challenge to those addressing environmental or social problems on a large scale.

Open source projects are optimized to deal with this, and since Linus Torvalds created Linux – an operating system as large, stable and useful as Windows or Mac – he demonstrated they could scale up rapidly to creating very complex systems with a fraction of the commercial resources.

In his landmark 1997 essay, *The Cathedral & the Bazaar*, Eric S Raymond explored what made these projects so successful and characterized software development as being either like a *cathedral*, from a small closed group of developers, or a *bazaar*, where code is developed over the internet in full view of the public. He had previously 'believed there was a certain critical complexity above which a more centralized, *a priori* approach was required. I believed that the most important software... needed to be built like cathedrals, carefully crafted by individual wizards or small bands of mages working in splendid isolation, with no beta to be released before its time.'

This contrasted with the approach he saw with Linux: 'Linus Torvalds's style of development –release early and often, delegate everything you can, be open to the point of promiscuity – came as a surprise. No quiet, reverent cathedral-building here – rather, the Linux community seemed to resemble a great babbling bazaar of differing agendas and approaches... out of which a coherent and stable system could seemingly emerge only by a succession of miracles.'[19]

Raymond concluded that Torvalds' approach was critical to Linux's success and went on to test this with his own projects, finding that it was far better at creating good, bug-free software. Torvalds claimed that his decentralized approach came about because 'I'm basically a very lazy person who likes to get credit for things other people actually do.' In reality, his approach of 'egoless programming' had broken Brooks Law, which stated that adding extra developers to a late software project only made it later, as the increased communication between multiple people only slowed things down. Instead, bazaar-model open source projects tend to improve as they grow in size. 'Treating your users as co-developers is your least-hassle route to rapid code improvement and effective debugging,' said Raymond, because 'given enough eyeballs, all bugs are shallow'.

Bazaar-style management

What then are the qualities of bazaar-style open source management, and how could this be applied to real-world problems?

A sociable, energized lead developer with 'an itch to scratch' – a problem they want to solve.

'It is not a coincidence that Linus is a nice guy who makes people like him and want to help him.'[20]

There's no shortage of people with ideas and, in open source, projects tend to form around someone with a problem who has made a good start. Applying this to real-world problems – it can't be enough that someone wants to address climate change in order to attract volunteers and momentum – they'll need to have done some groundwork to motivate people around them. In the absence of a pile of money to pay them, they would probably need either an existing project or an inspiring film, TV series or book around which to motivate people – something that would give them a position of experience and respect within the appropriate community. And they would need to be able to use that authority in an egoless way.

A decentralized approach to management – bottom up rather than top down.

'Why is the sea ruler of a hundred streams of the rivers? Because it lies below them.' [21] Lao Tzu, *Tao Te Ching*

For much of the history of Linux, new updates were being approved and added to the system solely by Torvalds over email with a philosophy known as 'release early, release often'. This approach prioritizes getting new features out fast, rather than waiting until a system is perfect before release. It shifts quality control from the central manager or maintainer, to the users and depends on a system for them to notice and fix bugs.

This works well with software with an open code base, but may be more challenging in real-world situations where the requirement is for something that works fully at first use, such as a hospital or transport system. Still, most businesses evolve over time in response to customer demand, changing conditions in the market, regulations, investors, staff expertise and personal interests and so on. This is particularly true in the media and information sectors, which may be why Wikipedia, the most famous non-software product to employ open source licences, decentralization and management, is such a success.

Raymond explains: 'Linus was keeping his hacker/users constantly stimulated and rewarded – stimulated by the prospect of having an ego-satisfying piece of the action, rewarded by the sight of constant (even daily) improvement in their work... Given a large enough beta-tester and co-developer base, almost every problem will be characterized quickly and the fix obvious to someone.' [22]

Many web-native publications run on this basis – people submit articles, news and content (often for exposure and a backlink), an editor approves it and adds it to the front page, thereby maintaining a little control over the process and in turn bringing a larger audience to the writer's work than they would have got on their own blog. Commenting on articles provides a level of feedback from readers, while a Twitter, blogosphere or Facebook backlash is the next step up from complaining about an offensive or false article – and publications that don't respond to this feedback soon fall from popularity.

With non-digital projects – such as campaigning or vaccinating millions of people – there will be problems emerging regularly, which in some cultures could be seen as a direct challenge to the management and be met with defensiveness. Under Torvalds' bazaar model they would instead be seen as the best way to improve the service, with the system designed to encourage and support this.

This might also require a culture shift in which failure was more acceptable. One reason people persist in solving problems in video games is that failure can be quickly laughed off, while coders seem keen to find ways to improve other people's buggy code in open source and all welcome that. Open source is also protected from collective failure for, if a project fails, the open licence allows anyone else to take the code and try again.

An open licence for the code – distributing the assets to all

'Perhaps in the end the open source culture will triumph not because co-operation is morally right or software "hoarding" is morally wrong (assuming you believe the latter, which neither Linus nor I do), but simply because the closed-source world cannot win an evolutionary arms race with open source communities that can put orders of magnitude more skilled time into a problem.'[23]

Co-ops are well positioned to apply open source thinking as the idea that all members can contribute to improving the service or product is central. At the same time, co-ops sometimes have tensions between management and members: management would rather not seek approval for every decision, while members need to feel the direction is moving as they want in order to invest their energies. Open source projects seem to avoid this conflict, even though they may have a few core developers – often just one – who will know the code and integrate submissions of updates. There may be thousands of contributors, but there is still a central 'maintainer' who has a near-totalitarian control over the direction of the project.

Arguably what keeps management responsive to their users/ members, and their members feeling their voluntary work isn't at risk of going to waste through bad decisions, is that with an open licence (like the GPL or MIT)[24] at any point anyone can take the software and 'fork it' into a new version they can adapt and work on. The core maintainer is just a maintainer, not a feudal overlord owning the land on which all else toil for free.

If it's felt that the maintainer isn't active or responding to users, then the project can split and a new version can continue separately, with a new name (as happened with Mambo becoming Joomla). This creates what is sometimes called a benevolent dictatorship – whereby the totalitarian authority of the maintainer is beholden to the collective needs of the contributing members, knowing they can leave at any point. The project maintainers, be it Matt Mullenweg for Wordpress or Dries Buytaert for Drupal, have the final say, but they have only got where they are – and stay there – by responding to user needs and motivating developers.

This same freedom powers Wikipedia: if the management began to let the quality of editorial suffer, a group of disgruntled users could fork the entire site and run it under a new name with a different approach.

Wherever the creating, storing and copying of digital information is the main building asset of an organization, the bazaar approach could be applied, and a co-operative seems a perfect vehicle within which to structure that.

Where it is more challenging to consider is with physical goods. It would be as if a branch of the Co-op in Glasgow didn't like the direction from head office and so could change the name of the shop and continue running – but with the logical paradox that such a split wouldn't create any loss of stock, money or resources from head office or the store, just a loss of human skills. The bazaar model is easy to apply to services, information, creative and intellectual property, where ideas, brands, content, designs, management approaches and so on can be shared, but is harder to apply to limited physical goods and resources (at least until 3D printers become widespread).

Understanding which parts of capitalism would best adapt to a co-operative open source approach seems less of a priority than replicating open source's success at uniting people's instincts to achieve a collective positive goal. Raymond calls this a free market not of cash but ego-boosting ('egoboo') activities:

'Connect the selfishness of individual hackers as firmly as possible to difficult ends that can only be achieved by sustained co-operation... Many people (especially those who politically distrust free markets) would expect a culture of self-directed egoists to be fragmented, territorial, wasteful, secretive and hostile. But this expectation is clearly falsified by (to give just one example) the stunning variety, quality and depth of Linux documentation. It is a hallowed given that programmers hate documenting; how is it, then, that Linux hackers generate so much documentation? Evidently Linux's free market in egoboo [ego-boosting] works better to produce virtuous, other-directed behaviour than the massively funded documentation shops of commercial software producers.'[23]

Version control – handling 'co-operation without co-ordination'

The final vital key to an open source project using the bazaar approach is called a version control system – a practical way to share the changes that any individual makes through the whole system. Torvalds created a system called Git to handle this, which powers GitHub, where the majority of open source projects are available. Clay Shirkey made his 2012 TED talk about how open source's version control system could transform society:

'A programmer in Edinburgh and a programmer in Tibet can get a copy of the same piece of software, each of them can make changes, and they can make changes after each other, even if they didn't know of the other's existence before hand. **This is co-operation without co-ordination.** This is the big change. Once Git allowed for co-operation without co-ordination you start to see communities form that are enormously large and complex.'[25]

It is easy to imagine how finding a way to implement a system for 'co-operation without co-ordination' for social and environmental problems could be transformative. To consider a hypothetical example dealing with climate change:

- It would start with an itch to scratch, such as making Britain 100-per-cent powered by renewables as soon as possible.
- A respected and charismatic individual or small group, with good tech understanding, would need to propose through their networks an approach to solve the problem. This could be, for instance, a comprehensive website to help people understand the incentives, technologies and cost-savings to convert their home, coupled with peer-to-peer lending to finance it and social media gamification to motivate and mobilize a large national team of people to promote and encourage households to switch. This group would then need to have a system to facilitate co-operation without co-ordination.
- By making all of the code powering their solution – from the database of green-tech installers to the infrastructure validating the micro-loans – non-proprietary, the project team can motivate the large pool of people who care about climate change to contribute work that will have benefit regardless of the success of the project. This could be data entry, resource-writing, infrastructure development, design or social media support. Mobilizing, encouraging and integrating such numbers would invite the bazaar approach

– invite and absorb submissions and trust (and encourage) people to improve on them if they are flawed rather than holding everything back and waiting until deemed perfect by the centre. As the public aren't used to 'beta' releases in the way coders are, and could dismiss something that appeared half-baked, the core team would need to stress this was a work in progress and only brand, design and push the core service once it was at a certain level.

- Given that such a project would be more service than product, a co-op would offer an ideal structure to allow the army of volunteers to share in the ownership and success of it, perhaps proportional to their input, while also tracking the management expenses.

- The bazaar model doesn't assume the core team will have all the answers – in fact, most of the innovation would likely happen at the fringes in unexpected ways. In many ways the core team aren't expected to be innovators beyond initiating the project – instead they facilitate a collective action to solve a problem and encourage and incentivize that with recognition and, potentially, co-op shares or jobs.

Conclusion

Bringing together the lessons about what motivates us as individuals with the methods to mobilize and organize large distributed groups of people to address the urgent needs of our planet: this seems our best hope of beginning change quickly enough.

This could come through co-ops, governments or the private sector. But as long as a private enterprise is funded from sources far removed from users, workers and those impacted by a product or service, co-ops seem to be the structure least corruptible by shareholder interests and distorting influences.

There is a co-operative alternative to capitalism, and it is working at a huge scale already, just without a co-operative structure. The challenge for the co-op movement is to apply these lessons and get closer to these communities. For those without a technical background, it may seem daunting. But people want to work differently; they want to co-operate and do work that solves problems. And they want to enjoy that process.

Eric Raymond sums it up thus: 'It may well turn out that one of the most important effects of open source's success will be to teach us that play is the most economically efficient mode of creative work.'

Nic Wistreich is a filmmaker and open source enthusiast

1 Noreena Hertz, *Co-op Capitalism*, 2012, nin.tl/1bRW2g2 2012. **2** Yochai Benkler, *The Wealth of Networks*, Yale University Press, 2006. nin.tl/11WYL6f
3 flickr.com/creativecommons/ **4** en.wikipedia.org/wiki/Wikipedia.
5 trends.builtwith.com/Web-Server/Apache. **6** w3schools.com nin.tl/16UnZAV
7 nin.tl/11WZ9Sr **8** nin.tl/11YHOZc **9** Boston Consulting Group, *The $4.2tn opportunity*, March 2012, nin.tl/11NB791 **10** Daniel Pink, *Drive*, 2010, youtube.com/watch?v=u6XAPnuFjJc **11** Jane McGonigal, *Reality is Broken*, 2012, realityisbroken.org/2010/11/06/watch-videos **12** nin.tl/11NBsbS **13** Daniel Packer, 'Zurker, Proof we were desperate', nin.tl/11YlGgo **14** nin.tl/11NBEbh
15 nin.tl/11YlRlu **16** nin.tl/11NBLU6 **17** Eric S Raymond, *The Cathedral & The Bazaar*, 1997-2000, nin.tl/11YJa6d **18** nin.tl/11NBVLl **19** nin.tl/11YJou7 **20** nin.tl/11NCdBS
21 Lao Tzu, *Tao Te Ching*. **22** nin.tl/11YJWQE **23** nin.tl/11NCqoD
24 en.wikipedia.org/wiki/Open-source_license **25** nin.tl/11NCOTZ

8
Renovating the house of co-operatives

Robbie Smith

1 Introduction

'Human life begins on the far side of despair' [1]

Jean-Paul Sartre

I think it is fair to say that there is a growing anxiety, worldwide, about the nature of capitalism. The argument that capitalism is the best economic system, by perpetually driving growth and thus raising everyone, over time, from poverty to wealth, is discredited by global economic contraction and the despair of hundreds of millions of people who cannot sustain themselves. This is certainly felt by the poorest in western Europe, who for decades had experienced some degree of comfort but are now unable to afford all their basic needs, such as food and heating. Millions more, while managing to keep a roof over their heads and food on their table, are experiencing decreasing pay, longer working hours with poorer conditions and perpetual insecurity.

Many of us desire to find an alternative to capitalism because we simply don't believe capitalism will ever work in the interests of ordinary people. Yet it is also true to say that there is no longer a dominant concept of an alternative to capitalism, which for a long time gravitated around a 'Marxist' belief in state planning. With the fall of the Soviet empire, it is widely accepted that tight central control and planning created a totalitarian disaster, condemned to fail. Subsequently, Marxism was discredited. The dominant view was that Western capitalist democracy was the final victor in an epic battle of ideology and we had entered into the 'End of History'.[2] This victorious belief lasted just 18 years, less than the existence of the Berlin Wall.

At the point of the Lehman Brothers bankruptcy in 2008, the global financial crisis seemed close to bringing about the meltdown of the entire capitalist system. For five years capitalism has lurched from one crisis to the next, as austerity destroys lives and livelihoods. Economists are again turning to Marx's analysis of capitalism, that it will eventually collapse in on itself, as a plausible explanation of what is happening. Coupled with climate change, global crop failures and an energy crisis, it feels as if we are staring into the abyss.

So this is the point in history at which we find ourselves, with life imitating art, where art is a mash-up of Dickens and Sartre. We are witnessing the ghosts of Existential Crisis Past, Present and Future: the loss of innocence and horror of utopian communism, the pending collapse of capitalism and the prospect of runaway climate change. It is enough to paralyze us with fear.

Yet, perhaps this *anxiety is the dizziness of freedom*.[3] In our lifetimes, there has never been such a collective desire to take a leap of faith and find genuinely new economic ideas. Solutions to a complex problem often come with a powerful visualization. This essay argues that the law of entropy can be a useful way to conceptualize economics. In the same way that a house can keep in heat, co-operatives can redistribute wealth. But the effectiveness of redistribution is dependent upon renovation. This is a story about the renovation of the House of Co-operatives.

2 The Law of Entropy

The First Law of Thermodynamics states that energy is constant in a closed system. The Second Law states that energy spontaneously disperses from order to disorder, to its least useful state.[4] Since entropy is a measure of the amount of energy in a system that cannot do work, the second law also states that there is an irreversible process in which entropy increases. Thus the second law is also known as The Law of Entropy.

A simple example is a hot coffee left on a table. It will always cool down and will never heat up. Now imagine a house in winter. Due to the Law of Entropy, inside heat will always escape to the cold air outside. However, it is possible radically to slow the process, with double- or triple-glazed windows, cavity wall insulation and loft insulation. In which case, the work required to heat the house is minimized.

I suggest that we can conceptualize capital flow in the same way as heat flow. Devoid of external forces, money will transact toward its least useful state. On earning £5, an impoverished mother will immediately spend it on a meal for her hungry family. Amongst the poorest, money circulates rapidly. Money for them is life sustaining. Whereas an additional £5 is meaningless to a billionaire – it is at its least useful. It has become dead money. S/he has no need to spend it. The fact that s/he does reinvest it, is a contradiction of capitalism, discussed by Marx, which we shall come to later.

Let's return to our example of a house and make it an analogy. In a capitalist world, the poorest are effectively homeless, exposed to all the economic elements. By democratizing trade and redistributing surplus value (profit), co-operatives can act as shelter. So let's imagine our House of Co-operatives. Currently it is desperately in need of repair. It is highly energy inefficient. Windows are draughty, walls are porous, heat is leaking out through the uninsulated, damaged roof. The dwellers never feel warm. Even when sitting near a roaring fire, they feel an icy draught on the back of their necks. To really utilize all of the house, they need to install a central heating system but there is no point until they fully insulate and draught-proof the house, otherwise they are simply burning money.

3 Insulation – a co-operative currency

The best method to dramatically slow the flow and loss of money to capitalists is for the co-operative movement to create its own parallel currency.[5] Let's call it the Co-op Pound. In our analogy, this is fixing the roof, insulating the loft and installing triple-glazed windows. It costs money up front but it will pay for itself, many times over.

A parallel currency is money that is complementary to sovereign currencies. Rather than replace them, a parallel currency is usually pegged to the sovereign rate and encourages the circulation of money within desired limits. They achieve this with simple economic mechanisms and capital controls. First, businesses can offer discounts to consumers buying with the parallel currency. Second, a percentage fee is applied to transfers from the parallel currency back to the sovereign currency. And third, if no interest rate is applied to savings, there is an incentive to spend in the currency, speeding up circulation and generating growth for participating businesses.

Most parallel currencies are local currencies. Some may consider local currencies such as the Lewes Pound or the Totnes Pound as quaint, with little impact on the real world. But local currencies have a strong history of counter-cyclic economic growth. Around 4,000 were created in the US at the start of the Great Depression in the 1930s.[6] Local currencies are credited with saving the Argentinean economy after the collapse of the Peso in 2000, the Patacones being a remarkable success, until the IMF forced the Argentinean government to close down the schemes in 2003.[7]

The Bristol Pound, launched in September 2012, is the first city-wide local currency in the UK.[8] It is run by a not-for-profit partnership between the Bristol Pound Community Interest

Company and the Bristol Credit Union.[9] The currency is both electronic and has paper notes. Individuals can purchase goods online or in store with notes or by SMS messaging from their phone.[10] Bristol Council is participating by allowing business rates to be paid in the currency.[8] Local producers within 50 miles can join the FarmLink initiative, which encourages a full economic life-cycle. It is expected that over 500,000 Bristol Pounds will be in circulation by next year.[11] Initially there will be a five-per-cent bonus on the first £100,000 of deposits into the scheme and there is a three-per-cent fee when converting Bristol Pounds back to Sterling.[12]

Another type of parallel currency is the online electronic currency such as BitCoin.[13] While PayPal is more a method of payment than an electronic currency, it has similar attributes to parallel currencies, as it takes a dominant role in eBay transactions.[14]

A Co-op Pound would be non-geographic and open to any co-operative business. It could perhaps be extended to social enterprises: charities, local community groups and micro-businesses with a co-operative ethic. When co-operatives trade with each other, a discount could be offered when paying in Co-op Pounds. The greater the discount, the more likely the uptake of the currency. This type of transaction could be online and hence very similar to paying with PayPal. It wouldn't necessarily need to be restricted to one nation. The Co-op Pound could be traded worldwide between co-operatives within a federation. Co-operative members could also buy from online co-operative retailers with the Co-op Pound. Again, this would be similar to using PayPal.

At the high-street retail end, the Co-op Pound would be very similar to a local currency. Individual members could pay co-operative retailers electronically or with printed notes. Discounts for individual members would again encourage uptake. Members of co-operatives could be offered the option of having their dividends paid in Co-op Pounds.

A percentage fee would be applied when converting Co-op Pounds back to Sterling. This control would encourage participants to maintain their balance and allow the currency to grow. Money accumulated in the scheme could then be used to invest in new co-operatives.

Imagine three scenarios. Scenario One is where a person spends £100 Sterling in a corporate supermarket. Much of the £100 will end up in the pockets of the shareholders of the supermarket and producers. Only a fraction ends up in the pockets of the workers who produced, transported, stocked and sold the goods. As the business model is to increase profits, this will ultimately be at the expense of wages and quality. So a hard-up person may feel they are getting value for money for their £100, but its long-term effect is to create greater inequality in society, at their expense.

In Scenario Two a person spends £100 Sterling in a co-operative retailer, let's say The Co-operative supermarket. In this scenario, there is a clear advantage over the first, as the retailer will pay surplus value back to its members as dividends. The retail staff are also likely to reinvest in co-operatives, spending their wages in the shop. However, whether the goods on sale are made by co-operatives or by capitalist companies will largely depend on cost (and perhaps a little on altruism). The Co-operative supermarket produces many of its own goods and owns many farms, but a high percentage of goods it sells will be produced by transnational corporations. So potentially much of the £100 spend would circulate within The Co-operative Group. But every pound spent on a corporate product in The Co-operative supermarket would mean more money leaked to capitalism.

In Scenario Three a member spends 100 Co-op Pounds in The Co-operative supermarket. That member has invested in Co-op Pounds not necessarily for political reasons but for discounts. They may even spend their Co-op Pounds predominantly on corporate goods. In which case, for this one shop, more money may flow to capitalist corporations than in Scenario Two. However, since The Co-operative supermarket is in receipt of 100 Co-op Pounds, they are most likely to reinvest in co-operative goods (because if they exchange back to sterling it will be at a percentage loss). So each participating co-operative is nudged into buying from other co-operatives with every transaction.

Getting a currency started is difficult and requires investment. In the Co-operative Bank, there is already an institution perfectly placed to develop the Co-op Pound and place enough capital into the currency to ensure its success. Perhaps they could consult with the New Economics Foundation. As increasing numbers of people embrace ethical consumption, there is almost certainly demand for an ethical electronic currency that would rival PayPal. This will be discussed later in the essay.

The currency will require critical mass and will need to encourage as many co-operatives to participate as possible. In the UK, this would require the largest co-operative, The Co-operative Group, to be a willing participant.

The House of Co-operatives is now fully draught-proofed and insulated. The occupants can now happily sit by the fire, without an icy wind grabbing the back of their necks. But the rest of the house is still cold and empty.

4 Capital without the ism

'Capital is dead labour, that, vampire-like, only lives by sucking living labour, and lives the more, the more labour it sucks'.[15]

Karl Marx

Now that we have fully insulated the house, we can consider installing a highly efficient central heating system – investment in co-operatives.

Marx points to contradictions in capitalism. *'It is therefore* clear that the higher the development of capital, the more it appears as a barrier to production, and therefore also to consumption...'[16] Marx argues that the success of capitalism leads to its downfall. Capitalism is very successful at driving production, leading to growth, but as it seeks to increase profits, it pushes down wages, reducing consumption, ultimately leading to collapse.

This essay asserts that, for the same reason that £5 'dies' in the hand of a billionaire, it makes the reinvestment of that £5 more likely, because the risk of loss is almost nothing. Therefore, dead money is the easiest money to invest. Consider an unemployed woman on Jobseekers Allowance. A 60p stamp for a job application each week constitutes the same order of risk to her as a billionaire's £10-million investment in a start-up.

All investment constitutes risk. For the co-operative movement to replace capitalism, ordinary co-operative members have to learn to be less conservative with investment of their living money. This is no easy task. Sharing risk evenly with some form of insurance can play its part. Another task is to teach members that money is never entirely safe anywhere, in banks, on the stock exchange or under the mattress. Risk is everywhere, so investment in co-operatives is the best strategy in the long term.

Where do we need to direct investment? I believe there are two distinct types of co-operatives that need to be created. First, there are large strategic federal co-operatives that will operate necessary infrastructure for the entire co-operative movement. An example would be a shipping co-operative to transport goods worldwide. Second, very small co-operative start-ups that are tailored to a locality or speciality can provide a vibrancy to the co-operative movement.

The democratic nature of co-operatives may also cause them to invest conservatively, since democratic representation can often lead to short-termism. Yet investors of large-scale infrastructure federal co-operatives will need to have a long-term view, as any return will be a long time coming. Therefore investments in these businesses will most likely be in the form of bonds and pension funds. The best way to convince members to invest is to show that there is a clear demand for developing a federal co-operative in a particular strategic area. This will indicate that any investment will be returned long term, and that risk is thus low.

The other type of co-operative that needs to be created requires a different kind of investment. It is in the nature of start-ups that many of these small co-operatives will fail. This is a higher-risk form of co-operative than is common today. Investment risk therefore needs to be small and distributed. An online site is required, similar to Buzzbnk,[17] to crowd-source funding for new co-operatives. In many cases, investors are not just buying shares but will receive dividends in future products or services. For example, Pants To Poverty are currently crowd-sourcing £100,000 funds in 100 days from their customers. Each year, investors will receive a 10.2 per cent return, 3 per cent in cash, 7.2 per cent in pants![18] This type of investment is perfect for small consumer co-operatives.

There is also a case for a co-operative peer-to-peer lending site, similar to Zopa.[19] Lenders can choose their own level of risk and lending is parcelled up, so that a lender's cash will be spread to a number of borrowers. In this way, the risk is shared and averaged out. Peer-to-peer lending can also create a sense of belonging:

'Borrowers often tell [Zopa CEO, Giles Andrews] that they would rather pay interest to Zopa lenders than a bank. They feel invested in rather than taken advantage of. Lenders enjoy finding out what their money is used for and being in control of setting their rates. Some even say it's addictive and fascinating seeing who's borrowing what and why, and will check their Zopa account several times in one day.'[20]

Rachel Botsman and Roo Rogers

5 The portal is political

At the same time as we install the central heating, we need to wire the house for electricity, so the whole house can become fully utilized.

When we consider a progression to a world full of co-operatives to compete with and replace capitalism, we are effectively talking about an emerging economy. Emerging economies need to invest in strategic infrastructure to grow. For the BRIC nations, this can be physical infrastructure, such as building roads and rail to transport goods. Whereas in rural Africa, where population is dispersed, it is the mobile-phone network infrastructure that is rapidly growing their economy, utilizing phones to bank and trade.[21] Virtual infrastructure is very cheap to develop in relation to physical infrastructure and is a very effective way to grow an economy.

A media co-operative is a priority strategic business that needs to be created for our emerging co-operative movement. Initially it will concentrate on web development. First, a co-operative online marketplace can be developed, that is similar to and competes with Amazon[22] and eBay.[23] Second, a co-operative formation and finance site can be added – let's call it Fantasy Co-op. This second site would be a social network to bring people with complementary skills together so they can combine and develop innovative ideas for new co-operatives. The site will help take them from concept to launch. As discussed earlier, crowd-source funding methods can then be used to provide the start-up costs. These new start-up co-operatives could then retail in the online marketplace.

The initial goal of the co-operative online marketplace is to get a foothold and survive. It couldn't possibly compete with established transnational corporations that dominate the online market. Based on figures for the ethical market in 2011,[24] if it presents itself as an ethical alternative to Amazon and eBay, then it has the potential for its share to grow to around 10 per cent of the online market. Online sales are quoted at £50 billion,[25] and just a fraction of this market would be enough for the co-operative marketplace to pay for itself and for the development costs of the Co-op Pound, which would be the preferred method of online payment. As long as it survives with a dedicated ethical consumer base, opportunities will grow further over time.

The democratic nature of co-operatives could help them flourish online for one important reason. As fast as online corporations like Google grow, the ultimate pursuit of profit leads these corporations to be ever more intrusive when exploiting their users' personal data. People are fearful as to how this data will be used and sold. Scandals such as Google's mining of unsecured wifi data, are rattling people's trust.[26] People want to know that their every click isn't being tracked and sold to the highest bidder. Becoming a member of a data co-operative could put users' minds at rest, reassuring them that their data will be handled responsibly at websites run by online co-operatives.

Progressively, the portal is becoming key to business and eventually politics, much as television was in the 20th century. Operating systems no longer make money in their own right but are a key to selling consumer products. Apple profits from hardware but also from tied-in sales from iTunes and App Store. Google is now selling its own tablets and laptops with Chrome installed. Play Store sells not just apps but music and video. Canonical, the largest company developing a Linux[27] distribution has Ubuntu One,[28] where music can be downloaded straight into your chosen media player. The co-operative movement would do well to consider developing its own Linux-based operating system, with an ethical search engine and a portal that takes the user straight to ethical co-operative businesses. This isn't as expensive or crazy as it sounds, as developing a Linux distribution is largely cosmetic. The problem lies in generating uptake and reaching critical mass. Again this may be possible by appealing to the 10 per cent of ethical consumers.

'The second reason why critical mass is such a vital ingredient of "Collaborative Consumption" is that a core of loyal and frequent users will be attracted. Whether it's Barclays Cycle Hire users riding around the streets of London on distinct turquoise bikes or a clothing swap blogging about the deals they found, these early users provide a critical mass of "social proof" that these forms of Collaborative Consumption are something others should try. It enables people, not just early adopters, to cross the psychological barrier that often exists around new behaviours.'[29]

Rachel Botsman and Roo Rogers

Another area of strategic importance is the physical transportation of goods. Imagine our success with the online marketplace, with many micro-co-operatives selling online. All these goods will need to be dispatched. Perhaps The Co-operative supermarket would consider expanding its food distribution road-haulage network to all co-operatives, as a parcel delivery service.

The ultimate aim will be to develop co-operatives in all areas of industry, from energy generation to shipping to waste management, so that each product can genuinely be manufactured, distributed and sold through a 100-per-cent co-operative life cycle. Generating online co-operatives is a cost-effective way to get started.

6 Happy families

So our house is now ready to move in its residents, decorate their rooms and arrange the furniture. There are two areas I would like briefly to consider here: nurturing new co-operatives and industrial disputes.

Bringing people together with the Fantasy Co-op will be one way to form co-operatives. The other way could be to allow for 'transitional' co-operatives: sole traders or partnerships that adhere to co-operative principles but are too small to form an actual co-operative. In some cases, innovators may want to start up a business from home or small premises and the work may only be enough for one or two people. Yet they may fully adhere to the principles of co-operatives. As long as they sign a contract, the co-operative movement could support them, so long as they convert to a co-operative as and when it is viable to do so. This is similar to a farm converting to organic. It takes up to three years before the Soil Association certifies the farm's produce as fully organic.[30] In the transition, the farm has extra costs but no extra revenue. However, the farm can advertise as being 'in transition' to sell at slightly higher prices than non-organic.

Innovation requires failure as well as success. These micro co-operatives are ideal for taking greater risks to test the demand for innovative products and services. It would be important to ensure that failure does not lead to huge debts and a bad reputation. Innovators will often learn from their failure and succeed second time around. The online co-operative marketplace would need to insure against a predicted rate of failure and provide guarantees to consumers.

The other area to consider is disputes. There is nothing about the structure of co-operatives that ensures that they will always have better relations than capitalist businesses. There are regular disputes between consumer co-operatives and their staff or producers. The Co-operative supermarket was recently part of the dairy farmers' dispute over milk prices.[31] Staff went on strike earlier this year at the Janlaxmi co-op bank in India.[32] On the other hand, a worker co-operative producing goods in high demand, with little or no competition, can be tempted to overcharge. Collegiate co-operatives (a loose form of federation) could be a solution. For example, imagine a co-operative running a rail route. A college could consist of a passengers' co-operative and a rail-workers' co-operative. Similarly, a media co-operative may be formed from a workers' co-operative (journalists and web developers), a telecommunications co-operative and a data co-operative (run by consumers, managing data from user interaction).

7 Conclusion

'Modern societies will depend increasingly on being creative, adaptable, inventive, well-informed and flexible communities, able to respond generously to each other and to needs wherever they arise. Those are characteristics not of societies in hock to the rich, in which people are driven by status insecurities, but of populations used to working together and respecting each other as equals'. [33]

Richard Wilkinson and Kate Pickett

I hope that what this essay may lack in academic rigour, it gains in creativity and imagination. I hope that it has entertained and excited the reader, as it conceptualizes the task ahead, maps a possible path and illustrates a future world of co-operatives.

If we are to be the architects of a world full of co-operatives, then our design must envisage not just structure, but also flow. Simply creating more co-operatives, in isolation from each other, in a predominantly capitalist economy, will result in more co-operatives competing towards the lowest common denominator. Only when the economic flow is fully insulated, can co-operatives flourish. At the heart of this essay is the argument that a parallel co-operative currency can serve to insulate co-operatives from the wild storms of capitalism.

Investment and infrastructure, necessary to any emerging economy, can be created with innovative internet co-operatives, that can embrace the ethical market and expand it, making trade not just functional but joyous. There is nothing magical or ethereal here: capitalist examples of these types of business already exist. Yet co-operatives have one powerful trick up their sleeve – democracy – that may lead them to dominate the online marketplace, as people seek to seize control of their own data.

A co-operative alternative to capitalism is possible; it can be envisaged; it is within our grasp. There is not one theory or ideology that proves its inevitability or predicts a coming utopia but a series of small actions that can take an ageing storm-battered building, renovate it from the inside and turn it into a wonderful warm home, fit for all of us to live in.

Robbie Smith is a writer and open source enthusiast

1 Jean-Paul Sartre, *The Flies (Les Mouches)*, Act III, 1943. **2** Francis Fukuyama, *The End of History and the Last Man*, Free Press, New York, 1992. **3** Søren Kierkegaard, *The Concept of Anxiety*, 1844. **4** Wikipedia, Laws of Thermodynamics, retrieved 3 Oct 2012. **5** For more information on parallel currencies read this 2011 New Economics Foundation article by David Boyle: nin.tl/17m2Sxu **6** Josh Ryan-Collins, 2009, nin.tl/17m35Rm **7** Richard Douthwaite, *The Ecology of Money*, Green Books, Totnes, 2000, nin.tl/17m3m6W **8** Josh Ryan-Collins, 2012, nin.tl/19hYw7R **9** bristolpound.org/who **10** bristolpound.org/downloads **11** Steven Morris, *The Guardian*, 21 Sep 2012, nin.tl/17m41VP **12** bristolpound.org/faqs **13** bitcoin.org/about.html **14** paypal.com/uk **15** Karl Marx, *Capital*, 1867, vol 1, ch 10. **16** Karl Marx, *Grundrisse*, 1857-8. **17** buzzbnk.org **18** nin.tl/18ZFK8O **19** uk.zopa.com **20** Rachel Botsman & Roo Rogers, *What's Mine is Yours*, Collins, London, 2010, p 165. **21** BBC News, 'Africa's mobile banking revolution', 2009, news.bbc.co.uk/1/hi/8194241.stm **22** amazon.co.uk **23** ebay.co.uk **24** *Ethical Consumer*, 'Ethical Sales Continue to Grow', 2011, nin.tl/11L4nwq **25** 'eBay leads the pack as UK online sales hit £50 bn', *Management Today*, nin.tl/18ZH8Io **26** BBC News, 'Google staff "knew of wifi snooping", report says', nin.tl/11L4HuQ **27** en.wikipedia.org/wiki/Linux **28** https://one.ubuntu.com **29** Botsman & Rogers, op cit, p 81. **30** 'How long will it take to convert my land to organic', Soil Association, 2011, nin.tl/18ZIdjv **31** BBC News, 'Farmers in second evening of protest over milk prices', bbc.co.uk/news/uk-18930618 **32** 'Strike continues at Janlaxmi co-op bank', *Co-operative News*, 2012, nin.tl/11L5nk9 **33** Richard Wilkinson & Kate Pickett, *The Spirit Level*, Penguin, London, 2009, p. 263.

Co-operatives and a sustainable future

9
Is there a co-operative solution to sustainable development?

Adam Fisher

'It seems to me scarcely open to doubt that a society with significantly greater equality in owning and controlling economic enterprises would produce profoundly greater equality than exists today.'

Robert Dahl, 1985

'Fundamental changes in the way societies produce and consume are indispensable for achieving global sustainable development.'

Johannesburg Plan of Implementation 2002, cited in Rio 2012

1 Introduction

Is there a co-operative alternative to capitalism? One possible way to answer this question would be to understand how policies of 'sustainable development' might fare through a predominantly global co-operative network, based on principles of economic democracy. The urgency to implement a fundamental change towards global sustainability has become the defining imperative of our current unsustainable times. If the co-operative organizational form could better incorporate the economic, social and ecological pillars of sustainable development in equal consideration compared to the prevailing capitalist interpretation, then an alternative may indeed be possible.

The idea of sustainable development emerged from the 1987 Brundtland Report *Our Common Future*, which has arguably been the most influential publication to date promoting a global shift in consciousness towards a more sustainable future society.[1] The report triggered 20 years of international political negotiation from the 1992 'Rio Earth Summit' to the 2012 'Rio Earth Summit Revisited'.[2] The report highlighted the hidden social and ecological costs of capitalist expansion occurring through global economic integration. As such, it supported the prevailing ecopolitical belief that a much better ecologically and socially reconciled society beyond the 'pathologies of modern consumer capitalism' was indeed possible.[3]

As Canadian academic John Robinson explains, sustainable development could be achieved through the recognition of the following:

'the ecological imperative to stay within the biophysical carrying capacity of the planet;

'the economic imperative to provide an adequate material standard of living for all; and

'the social imperative to provide systems of democratic governance that propagate the values that people want to live by.' [4]

Thus the concept of the 'three pillars of sustainable development' emerged to consolidate international efforts to redefine the nature of development along ecological, economic and socially equitable parameters.

However, despite the potential of the report, many communities of the world view sustainable development as a global management plan that erodes social and economic democracy at the community level while furthering ecologically unsustainable practices.[5] For a number of analysts, this is due to a 'business as usual' interpretation of sustainable development, emerging from advanced consumer democracies, which has failed to move beyond the neoliberal phase of capitalism generated in the US and the UK in the 1980s.[6]

The neoliberal phase of capitalism interprets and carries out sustainable development initiatives through existing economic practices of managerial and market efficiency coupled with technological innovation in order to produce a sustainable global economic system.[7] While market efficiency has the potential to deliver green technology, it has done so by hastening the erosion of democratic equality and ecological integrity occurring as a result of capitalist expansion over the last 300 years. As Atasoy explains: 'neoliberal policy advocates trade liberalization, the privatization of various forms of public property (including ecosystems), and subjecting all public and private life to a market-driven rationale of ever-increasing competitiveness in order to maximize efficiency for wealth creation.'[8]

Critics of the 'business as usual' interpretation view it as the latest phase of capital accumulation maintained through highly unequal power relations. As such, the capitalist interpretation of sustainable development is reinterpreted as an international policy devoid of a meaningful social or ecological vision of sustainability. The drive towards economic homogenization and efficiency using the promise of green technology has been pursued at the cost of democratic equality and ecological sustainability now felt at the global level. As a result, the 'business as usual' interpretation of sustainable development has favoured the 'economic pillar' of sustainability, subjugating the social and the ecological pillars to the logic of unlimited growth based purely on monetary value.[4]

With this in mind, the following section will draw on the theoretical work of Robert A Dahl's *A Preface to Economic Democracy* to present the possibility of a co-operative alternative to capitalism based on a *social economy paradigm of sustainable development*.[9] Co-operatives are able to incorporate the economic, social and ecological pillars of sustainable development through a cultivation of economic democracy at the community level. This paper will argue that economic democracy is able to address the three pillars of sustainability where the 'business as usual' capitalist model of sustainable development has failed to do so. The essay will conclude with a look at the UK co-operative food sector. Particular attention is paid to the multilevel network of democratic associations that connect the global co-operative movement together, representing the potential for a 'social economy paradigm of sustainable development'.

2 Dahl's theory of economic democracy

Central to Dahl's argument is the contradiction of powerful 'for profit' corporations, devoid of any internal democratic accountability, being cultivated within liberal democracies.[9] Dahl begins with a critique of de Tocqueville's historical argument for unrestrained economic liberty, made in 1856. De Tocqueville states that 'democracy cannot exist without an exceptional degree of social, economic and political equality, yet that very equality so essential to democracy also threatens economic liberty.'[10] De Tocqueville's argument is that democracies foster an increase in political and social equality which, cultivated over time, threatens individual economic liberty, because democratic equality created through majority rule is upheld by an increasingly authoritarian state legal system. To guard against totalitarianism, the economic sphere of liberty must be separated by law from the democratic sphere of equality. Thus economic liberty effectively becomes the guardian against despotism.

Dahl's critique of the above argument is that the logic of de Tocqueville, and those that followed after him, is based on a much earlier agrarian period in American history. Since then, the onset of commercial and industrial capitalism has generated vast inequalities in wealth, which have now led to vast political inequalities and an erosion of both ecological and democratic integrity at the global level. Thus modern industrial societies require a significant degree of democratic equality to offset the substantial social inequalities produced as a result of such expansion.

Dahl understands the erosion of democratic equality as having roots in the concept of individualized private accumulation based on the Lockean ontology of appropriation and labour. The freedom to work and appropriate resources to make one's life more secure is seamlessly transferred from individual citizens to large corporate firms through a mystical reference to the rights of humans and the legal personification of the corporate enterprise. As a consequence, international corporate capitalism becomes a symbol of economic liberty and democratic equality. Hierarchical structures become the promoters of a global sustainable society by maintaining the imperative of economic liberty and free-market entrepreneurship. However, in today's global economy, a major contradiction has occurred as the sphere of democratic equality, political rights and ecological integrity has been eroded through the economic liberty of large 'for profit' capitalist transnational corporations and their overwhelming influence on national public policies.

3 Community control over resource decisions

As Dahl's analysis reveals, the historical promotion of democratic values as an external element to the structures of economic organization has resulted in extreme disparities of wealth occurring at the global level. This historical process has produced a concentration of economic (and therefore democratic) power in the hands of a minority of the world's population. The separation of the economic realm has resulted in what Paul Hirst[11] sees as a global democracy of profit-seeking stockholders and shareholders, at the expense of localized democratic institutions that would be best placed to promote economic democracy.[12]

The imperative of the economic realm, and its central principle of unrestricted macroeconomic growth, is increasingly seen as one of the main causes for both social and environmental degradation as communities are denied autonomy over resource decisions at the local level.[13] Instead they are forced into a predominantly competitive capitalist culture, succumbing to the unstable forces of unrestrained economic competition. Even though the United Nations Development Programme (UNDP) has placed the blame for global social and ecological deterioration on unrestricted economic growth, it, the G8 and the European Union still insist on promoting the very same universalized model of technologically driven, but democratically devoid, economic growth as a solution to sustainable development.

Vandana Shiva views the particularized Western economic model as a globalization of the parochial interest of a tiny minority of economic élites, where sustainable development is promoted to mask the destructive forces of economic imperialism, co-opting the language of sustainability to place the blame for social and ecological degradation at the local level.[14] Poverty is defined as the root cause of social and ecological disintegration, and thus a 'prescription' for more economic growth via sustainable development initiatives is vigorously promoted as a solution to eradicate poverty and environmental destruction.[15] National-level policy-making on sustainability is redefined through corporate-led sustainable development initiatives, thus redirecting power away from local communities towards big business.[7] The disempowerment of communities places them outside of the planning process, and thus predicates them as an external problem to sustainable development projects.

For example, in the 2010 'IV European Union-Brazil Summit Joint Statement' the Brazilian government pledged to affirm the 'political commitment by Brazil and the EU to promote the use of renewable energies, including the production and use of sustainable biofuels'. They pledged to work closely with the private sector and interested countries on the promotion of sustainable production of biofuels through bioelectricity and other forms of renewable energy at the international level. Couched in terms of a green political economy to help sustainable development in Brazil, there is no mention of the social and ecological consequences of transforming vast areas of cultivable land into sugar plantations producing ethanol for the global market. In this respect, the creation of a green economy, vigorously promoted at Rio 2012, excludes a vast number of Brazilian people (approximately five million landless families) who are actively attempting to recreate sustainable development through the social economy. Brazilian social movements such as MST (*Movimento Dos Trabalhadores Rurais Sem Terra*) adopt the co-operative organizational form in education, health and the agricultural sectors.[16] Co-operative networks incorporate smallholder and family-owned farms in an attempt to redefine sustainable development as a set of comprehensive social and ecological values as opposed to a purely economic value that is implemented to satisfy and perpetuate the economic laws of the global market.[17]

In 2007, the MST released a press statement explaining that biofuel production could benefit Brazil if it was implemented through a smallholder policy of agricultural reform rather than placed in the hands of large estates. 'The interest in bio-energy could provide Brazil with a serious opportunity to reform its model for agricultural production, but instead Brazil's entrance into the biofuels market seems to offer little scope for protecting the environment and the livelihoods of smallholder farmers.'[18] Brazil is not the only country to have witnessed the marginalization of its indigenous communities. In recent times, a 'Clean Development Mechanism' scheme[19] in Uganda evicted 22,000 people from their land, allegedly at gunpoint, to allow the New Forests Company, a UK firm, to plant trees so as to earn carbon credits on the world market.[20]

As the above examples demonstrate, the Brundtland Report has been reinterpreted as the universalization of neoliberal resource accumulation, ontologically separate from the social and ecological realities of the communities that are to be subjugated to the logic of market efficiency, as both social and natural resources are transformed into commodities through the language of economic efficiency. All other alternative and culturally contextual paths to sustainability are portrayed as 'extreme relativism' and a threat to the stability of the planet's social and ecological processes.[21]

From the above discussion it can be argued that a fundamental principle of sustainable development is to readdress the social and ecological consequences of the historical separation between the economic and the democratic spheres of social organization. Understanding how these two spheres could be amalgamated through the co-operative organizational form may help us to understand better how social and ecological sustainability might be achieved. By using Dahl's argument for economic democracy, the following pages will present an alternative paradigm of sustainable development based on the co-operative ideal. The co-operative organizational form reflects a wider *social-economy paradigm of sustainable development* that moves beyond the limited either/or imagination of capitalism and communism, rejecting the false dichotomy that society has to rely on a centralized state or the global market to deliver sustainable solutions.[22] Instead, the co-operative organizational form has its historical roots in socially embedded forms of economic democracy.[23] If this is so, it can be argued that co-operatives are best placed to address the three pillars of sustainable development, where the 'business as usual' model has failed to do so.

4 Economic democracy, co-operatives and sustainable development

Corporate economic enterprises are normally structured around a hierarchy of 'command and control' principles. Transnational corporations also have a high level of influence on national policy formation. The presence of dictatorships inside firms operating from liberal democratic states therefore results in a fundamental contradiction within modern liberal democracies.

Within modern democracies, the limits of representative democracy are to some degree counterbalanced by a network of citizens linked together through association. Democratic associations are, therefore, not secondary elements of representative democracies, but instead are a vital part of a democratic system that takes equality as its central principle of social organization.[16] For example, co-operatives the world over adopt and cultivate democratic equality and participation as an internal organizing principle. The values of the global co-operative movement are defined through the International Co-operative Alliance as follows: '*Co-operatives are based on the values of self-help, self-responsibility, democracy, equality, equity and solidarity. In the tradition of their founders, co-operative members believe in the ethical values of honesty, openness, social responsibility and caring for others.*'[24]

As a minimum criterion to uphold the principles of democracy in an organization, Dahl suggests 'a process that allocates equal votes amongst its members alongside a system of effective participation where every citizen in the organization can have an equal opportunity for expressing a preference as to the final outcome.'[9] If these two processes are violated then any claim to uphold democratic principles is undermined and, as a result, associations of people can be said to be acting outside of the democratic process.

Taking this as a basic means to analyze economic enterprises, it appears that the 'command and control' model of business acts outside of the representative system of democracy, as well as of the system of democratic associations guided by principles of equality and participation. In this respect, it can be argued that the co-operative model of democratic association reflects the central principles of a modern pluralist democracy much more closely than corporate capitalist enterprises.[25]

According to the International Co-operative Alliance, co-operatives are defined as: '*An autonomous association of persons united voluntarily to meet their common, economic, social and cultural needs and aspirations through a jointly owned and democratically controlled enterprise.'*[24]

The co-operative movement consists of approximately one billion members in over 100 countries and it is estimated that co-operatives account for approximately 100 million jobs worldwide.[26] Hence the co-operative movement is able to connect to and promote a wider movement for community autonomy, responsibility, and social and ecological justice.[27] Economic democracy can be seen as promoting an alternative space, beyond the state-market nexus, in which to cultivate a social economy paradigm of sustainable development.

The presence of democracy in the economic sphere in worker co-operatives holds the potential to address collective concerns and needs in ways that 'preserve the resilience and integrity of democracy through social economic processes'.[28] If an economic organization is democratically controlled by its workers, and those workers represent the wider community needs, the possibility of equality and accountability is increased. With hierarchically owned corporate enterprises, community concerns are perceived as external to the economic sphere. If a transnational corporation (TNC) was negatively affecting a community through exploiting weak national labour laws or through polluting the local ecology, then the company is doing so by way of being virtually present in that community rather than being part of that community.[29] Community mobilization then occurs external to the TNC, within the democratic sphere of civil society, external to the economic organization. Community decisions and action are then presented to the corporate enterprise either through trades unions, the legislative system, or through direct action at the grassroots level.

Within a workers' co-operative, any situation that arises affecting the community is represented internally by the co-operative members representing the wider concerns of the local or regional community. In this sense, the democratization of the workplace links communities' concerns together to recreate trade based on a clearer set of ethics, defined through the seven principles of democracy and solidarity. As such, workers' co-operatives hold the potential to promote the economic, social and ecological pillars of sustainable development through supporting and co-operating at the local, regional and global level with individuals, communities and other co-operative and social-economy organizations.[30] The co-operative movement therefore helps to promote economic, social and ecological ethics where national policies have been eroded through the unaccountable power of modern corporations.

Indeed, by examining the UK co-operative sector as part of a global co-operative movement, it becomes apparent that each organization is part of a much wider network of democratic associations cultivating ethics at the global level. Co-operatives in the UK and the world over are cultivating what McMichael terms 'the universalization of difference',[31] attempting to integrate social justice through economic democracy in culturally specific settings, as an alternative to the 'purely for profit' capitalist model of global economic integration.

5 UK co-operatives and social-economy partnerships

Against the backdrop of industrial hardship and economic depression the Rochdale Pioneers established the first modern UK co-operative in 1844.[32] By placing their energy and faith in the co-operative ideal, the Pioneers, and those that followed, used community-based economic co-operation to resist the creed of universal competition. Since those early days of industrial capitalism, the UK co-operative movement has evolved as a social-economy alternative, to encompass a network of 5,933 independent co-operative businesses, and approximately 13.5 million people in the UK now belong to a co-operative organization.[33] In current times, co-operative organizations operate in a number of sectors, from high-street consumer-owned co-operatives to pubs and football clubs, healthcare, agriculture, banks, credit unions and community-owned shops, as well as establishing a co-operative niche in the UK environmental and renewable-energy sector.[34]

In particular, UK co-operatives are highly prominent in the food production and consumption industries. As Cato and Bickle explain, 'during the 2008 trading year, all but 2 of the top 20 co-operatives in the UK, ranked by turnover, were engaged in the food and agriculture sectors. Of the whole Co-operatives UK top 100 for 2008, 83 of the co-operatives were involved in food and agriculture.' This helps to establish a wide-ranging social-economy network from community land trusts and community-supported agriculture projects to community shops, country markets, co-operative farms, co-operative retailers, as well as consumer co-operatives.[35]

One example of a well-established workers' co-operative in the UK food sector is Essential Trading, a large Bristol-based organization established in 1972. Essential Trading owns a wholesale warehouse in Bristol along with two retail outlets in Bristol and Bath. Essential Trading (alongside Infinity Foods in Brighton, Suma in West Yorkshire and Unicorn in Manchester) are the UK's wholesale distributors of organic, vegan and vegetarian wholefoods, distributing throughout the UK and Europe, while encouraging the growth of smaller community co-ops. The organization currently consists of approximately 70 full- and part-time co-operative members.

Another good example is a co-op like Equal Exchange, which helps to set up and trade with growers' co-operatives and fair-trade projects in the Global South, mainly dealing in tea and coffee but also things like honey and nut butters. They only have around eight members – which demonstrates that smaller-scale co-operatives can also have a wide reach. They don't have to be larger worker co-ops like Essential Trading or full-on consumer co-operatives like the Co-operative Group.

The presence of an international co-operative network, reflected in Essential Trading's partnerships, creates alternative social principles to the 'purely for profit' capitalist economic model of global integration. The cultivation of projects based on economic democracy helps to promote a wider social-economy alternative to capitalism, challenging the command-and-control approach to sustainable development. The ethics of the social economy also reflect a concern for building social capacity through economic activity.[36] The partnerships created by Essential Trading and Equal Exchange reflect a wider multi-level social-economy network based on the promotion of economic democracy and the cultivation of individual and community sustainability as a guiding principle of economic life.

Through capacity building and a concern for community well-being, worker co-operatives promote sustainable development through a plurality of social organizations, including NGOs, mutuals, voluntary organizations, community associations, smallholder communities and other co-operative organizations. The evolution of a global co-operative movement, as part of a wider social-economy network, has given rise to a much greater and more equal distribution of economic liberty by creating the socio-economic space to cultivate the right to a decent and dignified livelihood beyond the limitations and the alienation of the state-market nexus of global capitalism. The promotion of social equality through a network of democratically run organizations cultivates a clearly defined stance on the integrity of local communities and their ability to maintain autonomy and responsibility over all the elements of sustainability. The economic, social and ecological pillars of the original sustainable-development paradigm are therefore given more equal consideration through the promotion of economic democracy, thus offering a sustainable co-operative alternative to capitalism in these current unsustainable times.

6 Conclusion

The creation of a co-operative alternative to capitalism, then, is realized through a *social economy paradigm of sustainable development*, which begins with a simple and practical idea: a democratization of the economic sphere to promote equality and participation from the local to the global mosaic of democratic organizations. Co-operatives promote the means to a decent livelihood, and the means to participate in the day-to-day running of the workplace, community and the ecology that sustains that community. Such an idea is not new. Indeed it has been the practice of many worker co-operatives the world over for at least the last 170 years.

Adam Fisher is an academic researcher and co-op member.

1 S Baker, 'Sustainable Development as Symbolic Commitment', *Environmental Politics,* 16 (2), 2007. **2** Sustainable Development governance has been a central theme of Rio 2012 alongside 'the green economy', earthsummit2012.org **3** I Bluhdorn, 'The Politics of Unsustainability', *Organization Environment,* 24, 2011; Baker, op cit. **4** J Robinson, 'Squaring the Circle?' *Ecological Economics,* 48, 2004. **5** V Shiva, *The Violence of the Green Revolution,* Zed Press, New Delhi, 1992; P McMichael, 'Globalization', in T Janoski, R Alford, A Hicks, M Schwartz (eds), *The Handbook of Political Sociology,* Cambridge University Press, 2005; P McMichael, 'Global Citizenship and Multiple Sovereignties', in Y Atasoy (ed), *Hegemonic Transitions, the State and Crisis in Neoliberal Capitalism,* Routledge, 2009. **6** V Shiva, 'The greening of global reach', and S Visvanathan, 'Mrs Brundtland's disenchanted cosmos', in GO Tuathail, S Dalby, P Routledge (eds), *The Geopolitical Reader,* Routledge, 1998; T Doyle, 'Sustainable development and Agenda 21', *Third World Quarterly* 19 (4), 1998; J Clapp, P Dauvergne, *Paths to a Green World,* MIT Press, 2005. **7** Doyle, op cit. **8** Y Atasoy, 'Introduction', in Y Atasoy, (ed), op cit. **9** RA Dahl, *A Preface to Economic Democracy,* Polity Press, 1985. **10** De Tocqueville (1856) is quoted and analyzed in Dahl, op cit. Dahl points out that, in addition to de Tocqueville's argument being based in an earlier agrarian period of US history, the 'democratic equality' to which he refers is that only of 'white male Americans' in this period. **11** P Hirst, *From Statism to Pluralism,* UCL Press, 1997. **12** Economic democracy as a global concept is described by Shiva as a 'lateral expansion of decision-making based on the protection of local community rights where they exist, and the institutionalization of rights where they have been eroded', *Monocultures of the Mind,* Zed Press, New Delhi, 1993, p235. **13** UN 1996 in T Doyle, op cit. **14** V Shiva, 'The greening of global reach', op cit. **15** S Dalby, *Environmental Security,* University of Minnesota Press, 2002. **16** As McMichael (op cit, p602) explains: 'The Cardoso government of 1995-2002 subordinated the Brazilian political economy to global financial capital in a late-20th-century context where 1 per cent of landowners own (but do not necessarily cultivate) almost 50 per cent of the land, while 4.8 million families are landless'. **17** JP Stedile, 2010, nin.tl/19oL2Le ; Via Campesina! (2010) smallfarmersbigchange.coop **18** MST statement 'Brazilian Biofuels: Who Benefits?', 2007, view at waronwant.org **19** 'Clean Development Mechanisms' or 'CDMs' are generic terms for a number of emission trading and reduction incentives emerging from Article 12 of the 1997 Kyoto Protocol. **20** World Development Movement, 'Forest Carbon Markets', 11 Sep 2012, nin.tl/120SUKd **21** R Irwin, 'The neoliberal state, environmental pragmatism, and its discontents', *Environmental Politics* 16 (4), 2007. **22** MS Cato, *Green Economics*, Earthscan, London, 2009. **23** MS Cato & R Bickle, *A Co-operative Path to Food Security in the UK*, 2011, http://ssrn.com/abstract=1970245 ; B Potter, *The Co-operative Movement in Great Britain*, 1891; GDH Cole, *A Century of Co-operation*, Co-operative Union, Manchester, 1944. **24** International Co-operative Alliance, 2010, ica.coop/coop/statistics.html **25** Although Dahl's pluralism was firmly within the framework of US-style representative democracy, his concept of democratizing the economy echoes the English pluralist critique of power held within a centralized state, or state-supported corporate centralized power. **26** 'Co-operatives in social development: report of the Secretary General', UN General Assembly 64th Session, Item 62, 2009. **27** ME Gertler, 'Synergy and strategic advantage', *Journal of Co-operative Studies* 18, 2004; J Restakis, *Humanizing the Economy*, New Society, Canada, 2010. **28** Gertler, op cit. **29** LH Brown, 'Organizations for the 21st century?' *Canadian Journal of Sociology* 22 (1), 1997. According to Brown (p85), in 1990, Co-op Atlantic in Canada carried a resolution to 'catalyse a network of interrelated co-operatives in all spheres of the economy, to counter the economic and social disruption caused by NAFTA in relation to the Atlantic region'. **30** Organizations such as the Soil Association and the Fairtrade Foundation are not run through co-operative structures, but are charitable organizations that fall under the various definitions of the social economy (see, for example, F Moulaert & J Nussbaumer, 'Defining the social economy and its governance at the neighbourhood level', *Urban Studies*, 42 (11), 2005; and G Smith, 'Green Citizenship and the Social Economy', *Environmental Politics*, 14 (2), 2005. **31** McMichael, op cit. **32** B Potter, *The Co-operative Movement in Great Britain*, 1891; J Restakis, *Humanizing the Economy: Co-operatives in the Age of Capital*, New Society Publishers, Canada, 2010. There were a number of co-operative organizations in the 19th century prior to Rochdale, but Rochdale instigated economic democracy alongside the 'dividend' system. **33** Co-operatives UK, 2012, www.uk.coop **34** MS Cato, L Arthur, T Keenoy, R Smith, 'Green and red?' *Journal of Co-operative Studies*, 39 (2) 2006. **35** Cato & Bickle, op cit. **36** Amin et al, 2002, in G Smith, 'Green Citizenship and the Social Economy', *Environmental Politics*, 14 (2), 2005.

10
Why we need to replace joint-stock companies with co-operatives in the sustainable economies of the future

Steve Mandel

You could argue that the joint-stock company is the foundation stone of the modern economy. It led to the large accumulation of capital that enabled major investments to be made, and undoubtedly fuelled the industrial revolution, at least in the 19th and 20th centuries, which saw gross domestic product rise in a manner never imagined before. Today the joint-stock company is massively dominant in both production and service industries. The total market capitalization of the main London Stock Exchange in August 2012 was £1,866 billion ($2,986 billion), and the Alternative Investment Market was a further £58.8 billion ($94 billion). Already predominant in production, banking and retail throughout the 20th century, the model actually extended its reach in the 1980s and 1990s in the financial-services industry with the wave of demutualizations of building societies[1] and mutual pension and life-insurance companies. The Big Bang reforms of the Thatcher years allowed the form to spread to accountancy and financial advice firms, which had previously been required to be unlimited partnerships. The London Stock Exchange itself demutualized in 2000.[2]

However, this period inevitably also saw unprecedented growth in the use of energy, renewable and non-renewable resources, which has accelerated rather than slowed down in more recent years. This use of resources is now considered to exceed the level that the earth's capacity can sustain by about 50 per cent, according to Dr Mathis Wackernagel of the Global Footprint Network.[3] While this increase in consumption undoubtedly had great benefits in terms of the standard of living of a large proportion of the population of the richer countries, the resources of the planet are finite and are now being depleted by that rate of consumption. This depletion will prevent those in poorer parts of the world from emulating those in the richer parts and, with climate change and rising sea levels, may combine to threaten even current living standards there. Furthermore, measures of well-being suggest that higher consumption has not resulted in greater happiness in the last four decades amongst those living in the richer countries.[4]

Joseph Fourier discovered the greenhouse effect of carbon dioxide back in 1824, and it was Svante Arrhenius who argued (in 1896) that the burning of fossil fuels could cause global warming as a result. Nevertheless, concern about the effect only began to be expressed more widely when actual warming was noticed in the 1980s. In 1972 the Club of Rome published its report *Limits to Growth*, which predicted that with 'business as usual' a number of constraints would lead to increasing problems and a collapse of growth in the second quarter of the 21st century. This was widely derided at the time, mainly on the grounds that technical progress would enable the substitution of scarce resources by others. Much was made of a few figures that were labelled mistakes, while ignoring the fact that the main conclusions were totally unaffected by those figures.[5] However, Graham Turner compared the baseline scenario with observed data for 1970 to data for 2000 and found a remarkable correlation.[6]

Few now question the danger of runaway climate change caused by greenhouse gases if emissions continue on their present trajectory and many are realizing that 'peak resources' are a serious problem for continuous growth of GDP. In 2004, some of the authors of the original *Limits* published *Limits to Growth: The 30-Year Update*, confirming the result of the earlier, 1972 study. While the details of when any collapse will occur under a 'business-as-usual' scenario can be a matter for debate, the inevitability of a major crisis in the coming decades is, to my mind, firmly established. The financial crisis of 2007/8 that continues today is but a fore-runner of what is to come. To avoid such a collapse we need to move to a 'steady-state'[7] or, more aptly, a 'dynamic equilibrium' economy as soon as possible.[8] The New Economics Foundation (NEF) considers that we have 50 months left to do so before reaching a tipping point in climate change that will make a catastrophic rise in global temperatures more or less inevitable.[9] Of course the timing of such an event cannot be placed this precisely but that is unimportant.[10]

Perhaps fortunately, just as we are being forced to face up to the Second Law of Thermodynamics and realize that perpetual growth is impossible, we are being presented with the proof that well-being, health and social improvement are not dependent on GDP above a certain level. Richard Wilkinson and Kate Pickett in their book *The Spirit Level* provide ample evidence of this.[11] They demonstrate that all manner of indicators of social and physical health are closely correlated with the level of equality in a society. The growth in GDP in most countries in the last 30 years has been accompanied by a marked increase in inequality, an increase which is, to my mind, intimately tied to the predominance of the joint-stock company.

In the joint stock company, ownership is often diluted to the point where oversight of directors' actions is not effective. This leaves room for the development of a culture that overestimates the value of directors to the company. While remuneration committees have ended the practice of directors setting their own salaries, the bulk of members of such committees are themselves directors of other companies. The culture is well established and has become more entrenched in recent years. (Of course it is difficult for any one company to buck the trend as they are competing for talent in what has become a highly mobile labour market.) As a result the difference between directors' pay and employees' pay has been growing markedly, without any indication that directors' performances have improved to justify this. The average total remuneration per year of FTSE100 CEOs rose from an average of £1 million ($1.6 million) to £4.2 million ($6.7 million) in the period 1998-2010[12] and the ratio between CEO pay and the average has risen commensurately.[13] While the ratios in the UK are striking and have been catching up in recent years, they remain lower than those in the United States.

This inequality is perceived by the general public as unfair. To quote the Hutton report: 'According to the 1999 British Social Attitudes Survey, the public at large believe that the ratio between highest and lowest earners in society should be around 6:1, a preferred ratio that has been notably stable over time.' While politicians can promise growth in the general economy as a rising tide to lift all boats, this perception of unfairness has not led to very active opposition. I suspect that, once the inevitability of a dynamic equilibrium economy is accepted, this quiescence will be at an end. As Wilkinson and Pickett have argued, a move towards greater equality will bring many benefits, and not just to those who are currently at the lower end of the pay distribution.

I wish to argue that while the joint-stock company may have been very appropriate during the rapid growth phase of the world economy, we now face a very different situation, where our use of resources will have to be much constrained if the collapse suggested in the model above is not to be inevitable, and when a marked decrease in inequality is desirable, and probably necessary. In fact, the joint-stock company has become one of the many obstacles to achieving a 'soft landing' from our current perpetual growth path, which, on the evidence of such studies as *Limits to Growth*, is leading us over a cliff. This is not just because of its contribution to inequality, as I set out below.

The stock exchange, even more than in the pre-1980 period, has growth built into the very nature of its operations. If the board of a company does not focus on short-term growth in sales and profits (at least, but often in dividends as well), then the share price will suffer and the company is in danger of being taken over by those who will. The key to board decision-making has generally become the effect of a decision on the stock price. (The easiest way to increase the size of a company is by taking over another, not by creating new products and winning new markets. This drives agglomeration, which reduces competition and favours large firms, often without adding genuine value.) For the present argument, the important point is that even if the members of the board are fully aware of the environmental and social damage of their activities, they will be punished for taking that into account if it does not reflect positively on the proverbial (single) bottom line (in contrast to NEF's triple bottom line).[14] Indeed, they are enjoined in law in the US to serve the best interests of their shareholders, which is only taken to mean their present shareholders, not future generations and not the wider community and pretty much only in the short term. This means, for example, that takeovers at what seem in the short term to be a good deal for current shareholders must be accepted, almost regardless of the long-term consequences. It also means that decisions which reduce immediate profits are seldom allowed, let alone actually taken, even if they would have great benefits for the wider community.

I should point out that the managers of banks are just as bound by this short-termism and narrowing of horizons to the stock price as is any other business. Any bank board that wished to be more 'responsible' in its borrowing and lending and in its risk taking would be punished by the 'market'. It is no surprise that they acted the way they did. As Chuck Prince, then CEO of

Citigroup, said in July 2007: '*as long as the music is playing, you've got to get up and dance. We're still dancing.*' Even those (probably few) who fully realized the dangers of the CDOs, CDSs and the rest of the alphabet soup of exotic financial instruments that have been created, had to take to the dance floor or lose their jobs. Indeed they still are, even after the collapse of Lehman Brothers. This pressure was exacerbated by financial deregulation and the decrease in mutuals and partnerships. The limited liability joint-stock company has now become the norm within the non-bank financial sector, which used not to be the case before 1980. It is therefore no surprise that they indulged in the sort of risky gambling that led us to the 2007/8 crisis. In Lord Turner's phrase – these activities are not 'socially useful', merely profitable to the traders involved, their bosses and, sometimes, but not always, to the shareholders.

The pressures on management from this form of governance prevent their taking any other path than the current truly unsustainable perpetual growth model. In theory, the board in a joint-stock company represents the owners – the shareholders – who could instruct them to act in a different way. Indeed, the trend of providing directors with a considerable proportion of their remuneration in the form of share options is designed to align their interests with those of the rest of the shareholders. However, it is not very likely that this will lead to the revolution in company culture needed and most quoted joint-stock companies have too diffuse an ownership to make it easy for shareholders to make radical proposals, let alone for those proposals to be carried through to fruition should they impact negatively on the share price. In practice, shareholders' interest is taken to be purely the share price and (but to a decreasing extent) the dividend, while the interests of owners of partnerships, non-traded small companies, social enterprises and mutuals could be very different. What is more, the board of companies quoted on a stock exchange are forced to take a short-term view of their strategy.

The activities of hedge funds and those who mimic them by taking short positions (selling shares they do not own in expectation of making a profit from a fall in price before they have to deliver) make share prices more volatile and increase the focus on the short term.[15] The advent of computerized trading has resulted in an even greater emphasis on the short term. Many trades on the stock exchange involve holding shares for a matter of seconds, though the average period for holding shares is of the order of one year. Shareholders as a class (at least as expressed by market sentiment and those who turn up at Annual General Meetings) no longer look to the long term of the company, let alone take an enlightened view of the needs of society as a whole.

This is partly, at least, the result of the way the pattern of ownership has changed in recent decades. This is very marked. The proportion of shares owned by individuals has fallen from 54 per cent in 1963 to 10 per cent in 2008,[16] and foreign ownership has gone up from 7 per cent to 42 per cent over the same period (the latter covers both overseas investors in primarily UK-owned companies and foreign companies that choose to be listed on the London Stock Exchange). Even the proportion held by insurance and pension companies, which could be expected to take a longer-term view than hedge funds, at least, has halved from 56 per cent in 1993 to 26 per cent in 2008. Most of these changes in ownership emphasize the short-term interest in share value as opposed to long-term stability.

WHO OWNS UK QUOTED SHARES, 2008

Rest of world 42%	Investment trusts 2%
Insurance companies 13%	Other financial institutions 10%
Pension funds 13%	Private non-financial
Individuals 10%	companies 3%
Banks 4%	Charities 1%
Unit trusts 2%	Public sector 1%

Source: UK Office of National Statistics

I conclude that the business model of the joint-stock company has developed in such a way as to be toxic to the expression of common ethical values in our social and political life, and to be one of the contributors to our inability to abandon a form of economy dependent on perpetual growth. That path is leading us towards catastrophe.

We therefore need as a society to move away from the joint-stock company model and towards forms of company that can take into account the longer-term interests of all their stakeholders, be they customers, employees or owners, the wider society and the interests of future generations. We need models which foster greater equality, greater participation and can give employees and the wider public a sense of control over their lives – all factors identified as contributing to well-being.[17] Co-operatives and other mutual societies are clearly of this nature. We therefore cannot afford to fail to make co-operatives central to the economy of the future.

Steve Mandel is an independent consultant and works at the Green Economics Institute.

1 The Building Society Act 1986 allowed demutualization to take place in this sector. As a result two-thirds of the assets of the building-society sector in 1994 were transferred out of the sector. J Cook, S Deakin and A Hughes, *Mutuality And Corporate Governance*, WP 205 ESRC Centre For Business Research, University of Cambridge, June 2001. By 1999 there were 68 building societies accounting for 18% of the stock of UK personal savings, 25% of the stock of UK residential mortgage loans to individuals (down from 80% in 1994), and a 40%-share of new net lending over the period 1997 up to March 1999. The sector was still important in terms of size – by the end of 1997 these building societies accounted for 2.8 million borrowers and 19 million investors; and employed 37,309 people. See Leadbetter and Christie, 1997; Treasury Select Committee, Ninth Treasury Report, 1999. **2** Despite this, in 2011, the co-operative sector had a turnover of £35.6 billion ($57 billion). **3** nin.tl/10TYbrV **4** See, for example, the work of the New Economics Foundation at nin.tl/122N8ro **5** U Bardi, *The Limits to Growth Revisited*, Springer, 2011. **6** 'A Comparison of *The Limits to Growth* with Thirty Years of Reality', Graham Turner, Commonwealth Scientific and Industrial Research Organization, 2008. **7** See, for example, the Centre for the Advancement of the Steady State Economy steadystate.org **8** See, for example, the NEF publication The Great Transition nin.tl/10TYNxV **9** nin.tl/10TZO8W and nin.tl/122O1Ae **10** For a discussion of this, see nin.tl/10U0QlB **11** R Wilkinson and K Pickett, *The Spirit Level*, Allen Lane, London, 2009. **12** Data from Manifest/ MM&K, 'The Executive Director Total Remuneration Survey 2011', available at: http://blog.manifest.co.uk. **13** To quote the Hutton interim report on Fair Pay (Dec 2010): 'it seems that chief executive pay for Britain's leading listed companies rose by around eight times between 1986 and 2010, suggesting an even faster rate of increase than in the US over a comparable period'; 'In 2009 FTSE 100 CEOs achieved a pay ratio of 202 times minimum wage compared with 124 times in 2000'; 'the ratio of FTSE 100 chief executives' median earnings to UK median earnings increased from 47 in 2000 to 88 in 2009. FTSE 250 firms have followed suit, if less dramatically, with an increase from 24 to 38 in the same period. It is noticeable that while chief executives of both groups of companies saw a drop in earnings in 2008 they rose again in 2009.' **14** Triple bottom line refers to 1 the enterprise, 2 the community, and 3 the environment; see nin.tl/10U1D5R **15** There are those who maintain that those who take a short position at least provide liquidity to a market that might otherwise lack it. I believe any benefit from this is outweighed by the impact of the resulting emphasis on the short term. **16** nin.tl/122PmqK **17** See, for example, nin.tl/10U2QKy

Co-operatives
and the wider
alternative economy

11
Co-operatives and their place in a global social economy

Cheryl Lans

For most of the world's developing countries, the 1990s were a decade of frustration and disappointment. The economies of sub-Saharan Africa and Latin America did not rebound economically in response to the structural-adjustment prescriptions of the World Bank and IMF.[1] Frustration with the World Bank and IMF led to the development of many co-operatives in Latin America.[2]

Involuntary unemployment is capitalism's most costly market failure and the demand for social services like the social-professional reintegration of disadvantaged groups usually cannot be provided solely by national governments.[3] An alternative economy often arises in response to unemployment. This alternative economy is composed of co-operatives and NGOs working on small projects for community economic development and ethical businesses providing services (camps, financing, daycare, media, housing, women's centres).[4]

Other groups working in the social economy include credit unions, fair trade organizations, women's groups, aboriginal and anti-poverty organizations, non-profits and some trade unions. This alternative economy is differentiated mainly by the types of businesses involved and whether cash is dominant or if barter arrangements are used. These alternative firms could replace many private companies. In fact Hansmann makes no distinction between a capitalistic firm and a producer or consumer co-operative, writing that the investor-owned business co-operation is nothing more than a lenders' co-operative or a capital co-operative.[5] This definition of a firm is a boon to those who have to debate the point with stubborn others that 'there is no alternative to capitalism'.[6]

Whether the alternative economy could become dominant depends on how successfully these organizations could integrate horizontally, how strong their relationships of mutual aid and exchange are, and if they could provide representatives to lead regional and national governments. Success in building these networks has been seen in Brazil, Spain, Argentina, Colombia and Venezuela; these networks of co-operatives have proved transformative for poor people and are not mere visions of future utopian societies.[2]

Proof that alternative economies are not utopian fantasies can also be seen in Europe.[4] The Emilia Romagna region in Italy owes its prosperity, low inequality, high social cohesion and high social capital to the six per cent of its workforce that are involved in worker co-operatives. In Italy, Article 45 of the Constitution recognizes the social function of co-operation.

Spain also recognizes co-operation in its Constitution – in Article 129, which reads:

(1) The law shall establish the forms of participation of those interested in Social Security and in the activities of the public agencies whose function directly affects the quality of life or general welfare.

(2) The public authorities shall effectively promote the various forms of participation in enterprise and facilitate co-operative enterprises by means of appropriate legislation. They shall also establish the means that will facilitate access by the workers to ownership of the means of production.[4]

In France, the model of a multi-stakeholder co-op or *Société coopérative d'intérêt collectif* (SCIC) was adapted from Italy.[4] An SCIC acts at the regional level to promote local development projects that look after the public interest in collaboration with local authorities and other partners.

The social economy was originally associated with utopianism and social change. Under the social-change framework, co-ops could provide services relinquished by the state while acting as agents of economic transformation and community resilience. The social-economy paradigm was adopted by the Catholic Church, and by certain European governments (French and Belgian) and then by the European Union (EU) in the 1980s.[7] The concept was revived by French academics Henri Desroches, Michel Rocard, Charles Gide and Léon Walras.[8] One of the reasons for its adoption was for its potential to address the crisis in the welfare state and the negative effects of globalization. Co-operatives were thus seen by some simply as another way of organizing businesses within the dominant capitalist economy.

Definitions of the social economy

Western Economic Diversification Canada categorizes a social enterprise as a specific business that produces goods and services for the market economy, but manages its operations and directs its surpluses in pursuit of social and economic goals. The social economy is composed of social enterprises, co-operative development and the third sector.[9]

- The social economy refers to all initiatives that are not a part of the public economy, nor the traditional private sector, but where capital and the means of production are collective. The social economy consists of an ensemble of activities and organizations, emerging from collective enterprises that pursue common principles and shared structural elements;[10]
- The objective of the social-economy enterprise is to serve its members or the community, instead of simply striving for financial profit;

- The social-economy enterprise is autonomous of the State;
- In its statute and code of conduct, it establishes a democratic decision-making process that implies the necessary participation of users and workers;
- It prioritizes people and work over capital in the distribution of revenue and surplus;
- Its activities are based on principles of participation, empowerment, and individual and collective responsibility.

Westlund and Westerdahl articulated three hypotheses on the social economy in Europe.[11] The vacuum hypothesis posits that the social economy can provide support when the public sector shrinks and the private sector does not hire and also shrinks. For example, in Russia, poor government support is supplemented by informal networks between neighbours, friends and relatives.[12] In Québec, co-operatives perform community services (environmental protection, etc) that are being offloaded by the state.[13] The influence hypothesis assumes that the social economy takes on the roles that the public service sheds through contracts (similar to the social-investment state). The local-identity hypothesis states that the social economy grows in the form of local initiatives as a reaction to the negative consequences of globalization. This is what happened in the Emilia Romagna region in Italy where social co-operatives provide healthcare.[4]

Mullan and Cox define the social economy as 'that spectrum of activity located between the public and private sector (and so driven neither by the logic of capital nor by that of the state) which is a form of economic organization aimed at addressing social need. Social viability and sustainability is placed on a par with economic viability and sustainability, with the two being interdependent.' They continue: 'In Ireland, the social economy is represented in nascent form by community-driven efforts to provide essential services which improve the quality of life and to address the gaps in facilities and services which communities have been deprived of but which are essential in terms of day-to-day living. A large number of social-economy enterprises constitute the adding of an economic dimension to work performed which has been historically undervalued, unvalued and unpaid: caring services, maintenance services, cultural activity and community banking. Services can be provided by and for communities on a basis which is more sustainable than simple subsidized service provision.'[14]

The International Center of Research and Information on the Public, Social and Co-operative Economy (CIRIEC) in Spain has the following definition: 'a group of private companies created to meet their members' needs through the market by producing goods and providing services, insurance and finance, where profit distribution and decision-making are not directly linked to the capital contributed by each member, each of whom has one vote. The social economy also includes non-profit organizations that are private non-market producers, not controlled by general government, produce not-for-sale services for specific groups of households and whose main resources come from voluntary contributions by the households as consumers, payments from the government and income from property'.[15]

An operational definition of the social economy would set boundaries according to the following criteria set out by Arthur et al:

- Ownership – locally based and owned largely by its employees (embedded in the community);
- Control – degree of power in decision-making and management control within the enterprise;
- Values – mutualism or reciprocal interdependence, not profit maximization;
- Product – preferably socially beneficial;
- Source of finance – majority of value owned by employees or local community; not totally dependent on grants.[16]

Sätre Åhlander looked at the role of the social economy with respect to employment, welfare, rural development and as a model of societal change.[17] She defined the social economy from a macro-economic perspective as the user-oriented third economic system beside the centrally managed planned economy and the market economy. The social economy then comprises activities for which users take economic decisions. Mutuality or close connections between producers and users are critical for the social economy. This strengthens its territorial characteristic – meaning local jobs and individual services. Also important is the growth of co-ops that have created opportunities for the socially excluded. The focus is therefore on the dynamic process of societal change and the role that the social economy plays in that change.

The social-investment state co-opting the social economy

Federal governments in Europe and Canada have turned to community-based processes and human capital investment to provide local solutions to local problems in increasingly complex and diverse neighbourhoods. This policy has been called the 'Third Way' by Anthony Giddens or the 'social-investment state'.[18] UK prime minister David Cameron's 'Big Society' fits this framework as well. This policy recognizes that competing in the global economy can take two forms:

1) A race to the bottom in terms of the welfare of citizens, or
2) Providing a highly adaptable, skilled and educated workforce that can respond to the 21st century's flexible, knowledge-based economy.

The social-investment state is a response to neoliberal critiques of social spending as wasteful and an economic drain. This has led the push to fund only those programmes deemed to be more cost-effective than welfare, income support and anti-drug and anti-crime spending.[18] The social-investment state has been criticized for focusing on children as the worker-citizens of the future rather than on retraining adults, for being gender-biased, and for continued adherence to the neoliberal macroeconomic framework (lack of concern for the environment and commitment to privatization of public-service work).

The Irish version of the social-investment state has been

called 'co-optation by the state. By promising limited funding and community consultation in statutory decision-making, the state converted activists into subcontracted civil servants'.[14] Activist organizations spent their resources on writing funding applications that were better than those of their competing activist organizations and needed to undertake legal incorporation, financial auditing and restructuring to fit EU guidelines. They had less time to spend on understanding structural problems and developing broader alliances, their radical language was not incorporated into funding applications and in most cases local activism did not fit the categories that could be funded. Organizations also needed to hire 'credentialed' grant managers who were not always community members.[14] Welfare and childcare needs were shortchanged.

Government support for the social economy: what would the world look like?

The social economy in Canada includes at least 175,000 non-profits. There are 78,000 non-profits with charitable status. These generate revenues of $90 billion annually and employ 1.3 million staff members.[19] The social economy includes 10,000 co-ops that generate $37 billion a year and employ 150,000 people. More recent figures on the non-profit sector estimate its size at $79.1 billion or 7.8 per cent of the GDP with 2 million people employed (11 per cent of the workforce).[20] Some Canadian provinces are more supportive of the social economy than others. Manitoba, for example, provided multi-year investment in community capacity and created a cabinet committee to examine all government activities through the lens of community economic development. Most childcare spaces in Manitoba are provided by non-profits.[21]

In 2002 the Canadian Community Economic Development Network allied with the *Chantier de l'économie sociale*, Québec's social-economy 'network of networks'. They lobbied federal politicians to create a 'Three C' policy environment:

- Multi-year funding ('Capacity building');
- Tax credit incentives to mobilize community financial capital ('Community capital');
- Policy changes and increased funding aimed at solving several serious problems hampering the effective development of human capital ('Competence').

In Québec, there are an estimated 65,000 people working in 6,200 social-economy enterprises, which generate annual sales in excess of $4 billion. The social economy in Québec includes co-operatives, mutual-benefit societies and associations. Many are linked to the Desjardins credit union movement. Excluding the Desjardins movement, and the two largest agricultural co-operatives, the Québec-based social economy has over 10,000 community organizations with more than 100,000 workers.[22] These organizations have developed new organizational methods and new market relations (multiple enterprises and partnerships, fair trade, alternative trade, networking), as well as new types of enterprises with new legal statuses such as social co-operatives or enterprises for social purposes.

Paul Martin, who became prime minister of Canada in 2003, had previously worked with *Regroupement économique et social du Sud-Ouest* (RESO), a successful collaborative venture between unions, businesses and community groups in a large rundown area of southwest Montreal. RESO transformed the area into a dynamic part of the city using the tools of community economic development and the social economy. As Regional Development Minister for Québec in the early 1990s, Martin made multi-year funding available for the core operations of RESO. Martin created a federal-government partnership with the Province of Québec and the Québec Solidarity Fund to create a $5-million equity investment pool for RESO development projects.[13]

Once elected, he announced that social enterprises would be assisted by:

- A fund of $152 million in addition to the existing small-business and business-financing programmes;[23]

- An expanded mandate for Community Futures Development Corporations;
- New funding through pilot programmes focused on capacity building ($17 million), financing, generating employment and research ($15 million);
- $100 million in credit and 'patient capital' for the next five years. The Fiducie in Québec offers 'patient' capital, funding product with no capital repayment for 15 years, available for real estate or working capital.[24]

Unfortunately a Conservative government took power in 2006, and not all of the promised activities were undertaken. The funding that had already been transferred, such as research funding, remained in place.[25]

The social economy and gender

Denyse Côté and Danielle Fournier wrote that gender equity became worse under state control.[26] Gender-based approaches and organizations present in the social economy from 1996-99 generated more total jobs, more jobs for women and better-paid jobs than after 1996 when the Québec government became involved in regulating and financing the third sector after the Socio-Economic Summit of October 1996.[27] Prior to 1999, the social economy was funded by 17 regional funding committees and women were represented on the management boards alongside provincial government employees. These boards ensured that projects with social ends were funded. The prevalence of women in co-ops is echoed in Europe where women find co-ops to be a convenient way to organize work, to share responsibility and to have democratic management.[12] Gender equity worsened when the Québec government instituted a gender-neutral approach from 1999, with the establishment of the *Centre Locaux de Développement* (CLD) and the *Politique de Soutien au Développement Local et Régional*.[27] The CLDs were service agencies for small business and only funded groups with the potential to be self-financing after one year; this ironically reduced the number of created jobs, led to fewer jobs for women and fewer well-paid jobs. Funded groups had to use business plans and reporting schemes that were not designed for their organizations and that may have compromised their initial aims. Community initiatives were no longer recognized. This outcome is similar to that in the Irish social investment state, as described above by Mullan and Cox.[14] Women were not given a place on the boards of the CLDs even though they were asked to voluntarily train those who took over the CLDs.

Researchers Louise Toupin and Nadine Goudreault have evaluated the social profitability of women's work and its contribution to community life so that it can be included in future definitions of the social economy. This measurement is necessary so that women's work can be accorded value in the market-based or currently defined social economy. Women's groups lost the opportunity to insert their unpaid contributions into the budget allocation criteria in Québec in 1999. Status of Women Canada funded a study that examined how the restructuring of the social economy negatively impacted the health and working conditions of women in Québec.[27] When Québec shortened hospital stays, women had to bear the burden of the transfer of care delivery to the home and had to perform more complex care. These studies have found that the shift to the social-investment state (rather than social economy), in combination with 'gender-neutral' policies (which are actually gender-biased) had a negative impact on women.

The social economy and a sustainable food system

The traditional definition of food security does not emphasize local production and ensuring community resilience or environmental protection.[28] A proper definition of food security should include three aspects:

1 Land tenure;
2 Environmental issues as part of sustainable production; and
3 Safe food from a consumer point of view.

In Vancouver, British Columbia, a coalition worked on the food-security issue. It included the Food Assessment Research Team and the Centre for Sustainable Community Development. Their vision of food security includes relocalizing food production, rooftop gardens and urban agriculture, direct sales from farms to institutions, and food-related social enterprises. They do not consider their vision to be utopian but rather consider it a viable strategy that should receive financial support from Western Economic Diversification Canada. The community food sector includes community kitchens, community gardens, good-neighbour programmes, co-op grocery stores, buying clubs and healthy food vending.

Vancouver's Forum of Research Connections claims that a social-economy approach to addressing acute food insecurity would improve food quality, support local growers and create jobs for current charity recipients.

Agricultural co-operatives provide sustainability. Although they are negatively affected by trade liberalization and the increasing concentration taking place in the food industry, co-operatives and producer marketing boards empower farmers, allowing them to forge their own paths.[29] Historically, co-ops have played important roles in the production, processing and sale of foods. Today, many agricultural co-ops are in trouble because of low commodity prices, intensifying competition, high capital needs, growing membership diversity and dwindling government support. They are often vulnerable organizations buffeted by international forces (often financial).

Multinational corporations use large-scale corporate agriculture that is increasingly short-lived, mobile and unsustainable; it reduces smallholders to producing cheap, standardized commodities for industrial food processing.[30] Dominant trends in the food business under globalization are: industrialization and subcontracting; global concentration of food sectors; effective and dynamic food distribution; marketing strategies based on product quality; and a uniformity of consumption practices in the international market.[31] In Canada, many large co-operatives in the grain, dairy and mushroom industries have demutualized.

The Cortes Island Shellfish Growers Co-operative Association is one of the founding members of the new BC Maritime Resource Co-operative, which was established to address problems of concentration of power in the industry. They provide shared services to small shellfish co-operatives (oysters and clams). They made large investments in research and development of the shellfish industry in order to support resource-based communities now facing lean times. Environmental problems faced by the industry are bad weather, predators and toxic blooms.

Co-ops in Canada are involved in the local provision of organic foods and are building an alternative food economy (for example, the multi-stakeholder Growing Circle Food Co-operative on Saltspring Island). The alternative food economy includes Community Supported Agriculture, food charters, the Slow Food movement, food box programmes and various NGOs. Their aim is to create a local and sustainable food system that improves access to fresh and healthy foods and gives producers a greater share of the consumer dollar. These initiatives also fit the social-economy frame, as a grassroots-based, regionally oriented federation of decentralized, autonomous and democratic enterprises building sustainable communities.[32]

Asia

In Asia, there have been strategic alliances of co-ops in production, processing and marketing for tropical fruit. The tropical-fruit industry has the classic characteristics that historically have given rise to large and effective co-operative enterprises – extensive supply, considerable shrinkage because of inadequate technology, and weak marketing mechanisms. Malaysian co-operatives work in consumption goods, tourism and agriculture. The social consequences of large-scale production of fruit for export have resulted in smallholders losing land to plantations owned by multinationals and large-scale growers, and in transfer of land from local food production to export production, resulting in food imports, labour and health/environment issues.

An alternative trade network has evolved in the last 15 to 20 years to offer producers and consumers a fair and equal relationship, which also provides environmental standards and healthy working conditions. This movement now boasts sales in excess of $200 million worldwide. In Asia, tropical fruits (mangosteen, longan and duku) are extensively grown by smallholders (over 80 per cent) and in home gardens, and can contribute to income generation. However, some fruit yields are low and not all can be commercialized. Asian fruit production and export are addressing issues connected to post-harvest, handling, processing and marketing infrastructures. The major issue is that the international market requires standardized, high-quality products.

Tropical fruits have become important to Southern countries as an alternative to traditional plantation crops like cocoa, coffee, oil palm, rubber and sugar that have low product prices. Consumer interest in organic and healthy foods has provided a stimulus to tropical fruit production. The increase in international tourism means that transportation is available, facilitating the exports of fruit. Between 1987 and 1997 the quantity of fruits such as bananas, grapes, pineapples, citrus and melons imported into Canada from the South increased by approximately 45 per cent, from 452 to 656 million kilograms. In 1995, 40 per cent of fruit imports came primarily from Latin America. Other significant sources are Morocco and Thailand. The most important fruit imports were bananas, grapes, citrus fruits, melons and pineapples. Other topical fruits include durian, guava, mango, mangosteen, lanalum, papaya, pomelo, rambutan, sawo and starfruit. Mangos dominate all other crops in terms of production. Other tropical fruit produced at significant levels are pineapples, avocados and papaya.[33]

Africa

In Africa, co-ops have been making an impact on land tenure and microcredit issues for the benefit of female farmers. In Nigeria, women make up between 60 and 80 per cent of the agricultural labour force, depending on the region, and produce two-thirds of the country's food crops. As elsewhere in Africa, however, extension services have focused on men and their farm production needs and women have had difficulties accessing land and credit. When women do own land, the land holding tends to be smaller and located in more marginal areas. Since rural women have less access than men to credit, this limits their ability to purchase seeds, fertilizers and other inputs needed to adopt new farming techniques.

Only five per cent of the resources provided through extension services in Africa are available to women, notes Marie Randriamamonjy, Director of the FAO's Women in Development Service: 'Although, in some cases, particularly in food production, African women handled 80 per cent of the work, of total extension agents at work in Africa today, only 17 per cent are women.' There has been some growth in the number of non-governmental organizations and women's associations involving or working with rural women. Sometimes these are mixed organizations, but frequently, rural women prefer to belong to groups run by women. Traditional credit programmes have failed to reach these farmers. Microcredit as bottom-up rather than top-down financing has potential for sustainable and gender-neutral rural financial systems.

Co-operatives offer an alternative model

Mondragon is both a corporation and a federation of worker co-operatives but it is also the largest business group in the Basque region and the seventh largest in Spain. Mondragon has a pay cap in which the highest-paid worker can only earn 6.5 times more than the lowest paid; it has 85,000 members, of which 43 per cent are women. This one company reduces gender and income inequality in the Basque region. Mondragon shows how co-operatives growing to large sizes in many economic sectors can be transformative. Similarly, La Cooperativa Humar-Marinaleda, a farmer co-operative in the Andalusian region of southern Spain, pays all of its workers the same 47 euros per day and they earn almost twice Spain's minimum wage. Jobs are rotated and their motto is 'To work less so that all may work'. Contrast this to the situation in many developed countries where many high-ranking people are proud to have several jobs, including paid board memberships, even at times when unemployment figures are very high. The Marinaleda council implemented measures to prevent the real-estate speculation which undermined the rest of the Spanish economy. The co-operative has also provided education and has an action squad instead of a legislative body.[34]

Co-operatives all over the world offer an alternative model of social organization that addresses some of the core problems within contemporary capitalism such as inadequate employment, global inequality and food insecurity.[6] In the past they offered another way of organizing businesses within a predominantly capitalist economy, but as the inherent weaknesses of capitalism are becoming more apparent, the co-operative alternative is gaining strength.

Cheryl Lans is a Canadian academic and author.

1 D Rodrik, 'Development strategies for the 21st century', World Bank Conference on Development Economics 2000, nin.tl/15lh8tK ; D Rodrik, 'Trade policy reform as institutional reform', in BM Hoekman, P English and A Mattoo (eds), *Development, Trade, and the WTO: A Handbook*, World Bank, 2002, nin.tl/15lhBfq **2** E Miller, 'Other economies are possible', *Dollars & Sense*, 2006, alternet.org/story/40339/
3 José Luis Monzón Campos, 'Contributions of the social economy to the general interest', *Annals of Public and Cooperative Economics*, 68 (3), 1997. **4** H Corcoran & D Wilson, 'The worker co-operative movements in Italy, Mondragon and France', 2010, nin.tl/10U538P **5** H Hansmann, 'Cooperative Firms in Theory and Practice', *Finnish Journal of Business Economics*, 4, 1999. **6** R Wolff, 'Yes, there is an alternative to capitalism: Mondragon shows the way', *The Guardian*, 24 June 2012, nin.tl/15liZic **7** F Moulaert & O Ailenei, 'Social economy, third sector and solidarity relations',

Urban Studies 42(11), 2005; D Côté & D Fournier, 'Is Quebec's "Third Way" gender-sensitive?' *Making Waves* 16 (3), 2005; Jean-Marc Fontan & E Shragge, *Social Economy: International Debates and Perspectives*, Black Rose Books, 2000. **8** J Laville, B Levesque & M Mendell, 'Diverse Approaches and Practices in Europe and Canada', in *The Social Economy: Building Inclusive Economies*, OECD, 2008. **9** F Salkie, 'Defining the Social Economy', *Access West*, Apr-Jun 2005. **10** N Neamtan, 'The Social and Solidarity Economy', background paper for symposium, Citizenship and Globalization: Exploring Participation and Democracy in a Global Context, Langara College, Vancouver, 14-16 Jun 2002. **11** H Westlund & S Westerdahl, 'Contribution of the social economy to local employment', Swedish Institute for Social Economy (SISE), Östersund, 1997. **12** A-M Sätre Åhlander, 'Women and the social economy in transitional Russia', *Annals of Public and Cooperative Economics*, 71 (3), 2000; Unfortunately Sätre Åhlander, 2000 does not completely understand what social capital is and links it only to the formal economy. **13** M Lewis, 'CED and the social economy break through onto the federal agenda', *Making Waves*, Spring 2004 **14** L Cox & C Mullan, 'Social movements never died', International Sociological Association Social Movements Conference, Nov 2001, http://eprints.nuim.ie/1529/ **15** Monzón Campos, op cit; R Chaves & JL Monzón, 'Las cooperatives en las modernas economías de Mercado', *Rev Economistas*, 83, 2000. **16** L Arthur, M Scott-Cato, T Keenoy & R Smith, 'Developing an operational definition of the social economy', *Journal of Cooperative Studies*, 36, 2003. **17** AM Sätre Åhlander, 'The social economy: new co-operatives and public sector', *Annals of Public and Cooperative Economics*, 72 (3), 2001. **18** D Perkins, L Nelms & P Smyth, 'Beyond Neo-liberalism: The Social Investment State?' *Just Policy*, 38, Dec 2005, nin.tl/19wl1sa **19** J Quarter, L Mook & BJ Richmond, 'What is the Social Economy?' *CUCS Research Bulletins* 13, Mar 2003. **20** S Geller & L Salamon, 'Non-profit advocacy: What do we know?' John Hopkins Center for Civil Society Studies, 2007, nin.tl/15lmKnY **21** S Prentice & M McCracken, *Time for Action*, Child Care Coalition of Manitoba, 2004. **22** N Neamtan & R Downing, 'Social economy and community economic development in Canada', Montréal, 2005, nin.tl/19wJuPf **23** ACCORD, 'Canadian PM announces big $$$ for social economy', 2003, accord. org.au **24** L Favreau, 'Entreprises collectives, les enjeux sociopolitiques et territoriaux de la coopération et de l'économie sociale', PUQ, 2008, nin.tl/15lnQQz **25** J Smith & A McKitrick, 'Current conceptualizations of the social economy in the Canadian context', University of Victoria, 2010, nin.tl/19wKCT9 **26** Côté & Fournier, op cit. **27** Status of Women Canada, 'Who will be responsible for providing care?' 2004, swc-cfc.gc.ca **28** The World Food Summit definition of food security: 'Food security exists when all people, at all times, have physical and economic access to sufficient, safe and nutritious food for a healthy and active life,' 1996. **29** W Moran, G Blunden & A Bradly, 'Empowering family farms through cooperatives and producer marketing boards', *Economic Geography*, 72, 1996 ; D Côté, M Fulton & J Gibbings, 'Canadian Agricultural Cooperatives', Canadian Cooperative Association, 2000. **30** R Nigh, 'Corporate versus smallholder farming', *Urban Anthropology* 28, 1999. **31** M-C Renard, 'The interstices of globalization: the example of fair coffee', *Sociologia Ruralis* 39, 1999. **32** P Wilkinson & J Quarter, 'A theoretical framework for community-based development', *Economic and Industrial Democracy*, 16 (4), 1995. **33** FAO, *Commodity Market Review 1999-2000*, Rome, 2001, nin.tl/19wNpLY **34** Presseurop, 'Workers' cooperative defies crisis', 2012, nin.tl/15lqTYW

12
Experiments in solidarity economics – alternative financial organizations in France and Italy

Arianna Lovera

Introduction

The capitalist system (and its financial version in particular) currently faces an obvious crisis. Nevertheless, it remains unclear whether alternative models are practical or, in other words, referring to a slogan which has become well known, whether 'another economic system is possible'. While making reference to ongoing debates in the fields of sociology, economics, political science and philosophy which critique capitalism and propose practically viable alternatives, I will examine practices I observed in three organizations (Banca Etica and MAG6[1] in Italy, and La Nef[2] in France) dedicated to the construction of an 'alternative finance'.

All three organizations aspire to build 'another kind of finance', implying an aspiration for a type of finance which tries to be different from the current 'speculative finance'. This ambition seems to be rich in critical and transformative potential, since it touches on a particularly controversial aspect of the present capitalist system: the growing importance of financial operations, a process also known as 'financialization of the economy'.

'Alternative' finance is itself defined as 'ethical' (Banca Etica), 'critical' (MAG6) or 'solidarity' (La Nef), which can nevertheless all be considered part of what J-L Laville and AD Cattani call 'solidarity economics'.[3] This term refers to organizations of producers, consumers and savers 'which value the notion of solidarity, as opposed to that of competitive individualism which characterizes the dominant economic behaviour in capitalist societies'.[4]

This essay will discuss a theoretical analysis of the possible alternatives to capitalism against empirical data from a survey covering the daily practices in the field of alternative finance. In the first part, I will examine the theoretical analyses of possible critiques of capitalism, and I will also describe recent transformations within capitalism towards the abovementioned 'financialization of the economy'. I will then deal with the sociological and economic theories concerning the possibility of building alternative concepts and practices in the financial sector. In the second, I will describe the observed daily activities carried out by employees at Banca Etica, MAG6 and La Nef. In particular, I will focus on the criteria adopted for the granting of loans, which include both banking and social/environmental criteria, and on the difficulties these organizations face in finding a balance between solidarity principles and market constraints – between ethical financial activity and customers' financial needs.

The engine of financial capitalism

In *The New Spirit of Capitalism*, Boltanski and Chiapello employ a 'minimal definition' of capitalism, according to which this system would coincide with the process of unlimited accumulation of capital by formally peaceful means.[5] Capitalism, therefore, would not hold absolute power over the actors it involves in its logic – on the contrary, it would have to avoid all forms of explicit violence (at least in its centre) in order to show itself as a legitimate system. This argument is similar to the one raised by Marx, who noted that capitalism, once established, no longer needs to use brute force, which instead characterizes its initial installation.[6]

The 'mega-engine' that the Italian sociologist Luciano Gallino designates as *'finanzcapitalismo'* coincides with recently developed devices aimed at 'maximizing and accumulating in the form of capital and power the value extracted from both the greatest number of people and ecosystems'.[7]

Banks are the prominent institutions in the *finanzcapitalismo* model. In fact, their operations are not limited to credit, but extend to a variety of fields involving a high degree of interdependence with other actors. Another sector of activity essential to the functioning of *finanzcapitalismo* is 'shadow finance', which includes 'derivative products' and those companies created by banks in order to manage off-balance activities.

Institutional investors such as pension funds, mutual investment funds, insurance companies and hedge funds operate at the crossroads of these two elements (the banking system and shadow finance). Since the 1980s, these three dimensions have maintained the daily exchanges of money through many channels, in hundreds of billions of dollars or euros.[7]

Another recent change in capitalism is the fact that it has become technically possible – thanks to internet and computer technology – to exchange information around the world at ever-higher speeds, as well as to base decisions once regarded as 'political' on quantitative data, using decision-making techniques supported by dedicated software.[8] In addition, there is increasing 'capital liberation', through both opening of borders and lack of control over the nature of market exchanges.

Nevertheless, for *finanzcapitalismo* to emerge as the dominant economic model, it would require that politics abdicate its role of steering and even governing the economy. This seems to have occurred, with political parties identifying their goals with those of financial capitalism, making it the dominant political system at the international level.[9] Indeed, from the early 1980s, boundaries between economics and politics have become more permeable due to the continuous exchange of personnel ('revolving doors') and shared language, patterns of interpretation, as well as sensitivity to certain issues and insensitivity to others.[7]

Problems for critical perspectives

Reasons for opposing capitalism in a critical and antagonistic way are not lacking. Nonetheless, no radical reversal of this system is on the horizon yet, with critical actors at the margins of society. In fact, many of capitalism's subjects seem to be unable to put into place a radical transformation of this model, finding themselves in one of two conditions (or both) that make them unable to perform effective, critical activity: either economic powerlessness or psychological submissiveness. Moreover, current capitalism is further supported by the neoliberal ideology that justifies it. This promotes the need for growth as well as a faith in self-regulating markets and the privatization of public goods as the only effective ways to avoid government bankruptcy.[7] In addition, *finanzcapitalismo* seems to be able to generate the anthropological type to work in this system – namely the avid speculator on the one hand, and the indebted guilty individual on the other.[10]

As a result, any counter-movement[11] and all instances which aspire to be critical of the present capitalist system face the challenge of proposing a different financial performance from the one put forward by liberal ideology, establishing therefore an alternative anthropogenesis. Given the fact that financial aspects are crucial in modern capitalism, it seems essential for an effective critical theory to provide alternative ideas and practices specifically in the field of finance. Beyond its purely technical dimension, the sector of alternative finance can thus be considered as rich in critical and emancipating potential.

However, the capitalist model of finance has so deeply shaped public imagination that the expression 'ethical' or 'solidarity' finance may sound oxymoronic. Indeed, actors involved in this sector deal with the difficult task of refusing certain characteristics of capitalism while assuming some of its principles as well. For instance, 'they contest subjecting the whole economy to the general aim of maximizing profits without considering any extra-economic criteria' (such as environmental factors or working conditions); however, at the same time 'they also share the capitalist focus on freedom of private enterprises and the idea that economic activity should be profitable'.[12]

These organizations seem thus to accept taking part in a market economy while challenging its capitalist aspect. Indeed, they give the impression of having incorporated the distinction proposed by the Italian economists Luigino Bruni and Stefano Zamagni between capitalist markets and civil markets.[13] Both these models belong to the market economy, and therefore are based on 'division of labour, on the organization of economic activity towards development (and therefore towards accumulation), and on the freedom of private enterprise'.[12] Starting from these principles characterizing any market economy, capitalist and civic markets differ from each other. Under capitalism, productive activity as a whole is directed towards a single goal – namely, the maximization of profit. By contrast, the civil-market model implies a kind of competition that does not aim at the destruction of competitors.[14]

Any thought or practice that aspires to challenge the social reality is at risk of 'institutional isomorphism', if we accept the assumption of the impossibility of a radical critique or exit option. This is especially true with regard to alternative finance, because it aims to contest some aspects of capitalism; yet at the same time it is part of a market economy and thus subject to the identical international regulation system which applies to 'capitalist' banks. Institutional isomorphism would propel alternative finance actors towards the model of capitalist enterprises, these two systems themselves converging on a single form characterized by the general implementation of industrial management techniques.[8] Indeed, the principles underlying the field of alternative finance are linked both to characteristics of capitalism (for example, the emphasis on free individual action and the concept of profitability) and to elements of anti-capitalist critique (such as the refusal of profit as the main goal of financial transactions or the importance given to relational capital among the guarantees required in loan-granting procedures).[12]

The field of alternative finance in Italy and France

As Bruno Frère pointed out, solidarity or ethical finance seems to be based on a 'grammar' (that is, social rules for co-ordinating actors' behaviours) similar to the one that characterizes workers' mutual help systems.[15] However, this sector is highly heterogeneous. For instance, in Italy, both the co-operatives MAG and Banca Prossima claim to be part of it. The MAG consider money to be a tool for reaching a wider social purpose in order to develop equitable relationships, not only between individuals but also between individuals and the social/natural environment. In contrast, Banca Prossima appears to be devoid of any 'critical' reference, being identified by its founders as a resource to attract new customers to the group 'Intesa Sanpaolo'.

I will refer in particular to the activity carried out by the co-operative 'MAG6' – the arm of MAG in Reggio Emilia – by the bank 'Banca Etica' in Italy, and by the financial company 'La Nef' in France. The choice of these three organizations is justified primarily by three criteria:

1　They fulfil the basic functions of banks, namely the collecting of savings and granting of loans.
2　They are heterogeneous in terms of legal form and size. Banca Etica is a bank, while MAG6 and La Nef have not taken on that legal form; Banca Etica and La Nef are larger organizations spread throughout their national territory, whereas MAG6 is a small, locally oriented actor.

3 They implement the main principles of solidarity or ethical finance, namely transparency concerning the final destination of the money collected (in terms of capital, savings deposits, etc) and adoption of both economic and social/environmental lending criteria.

As a consequence, I have chosen not to include the Italian banks 'Banche di Credito Cooperativo' and the French bank 'Crédit Cooperatif' in my study – despite the fact that they have close or even very close ties with Banca Etica and La Nef – because they seem to belong to the social-finance sector rather than to the field of alternative finance. Although their legal forms are that of 'co-operative banks', they only very marginally apply the principles of transparency with regard to their money's final destination and the adoption of both banking and ethical criteria in loan procedures.[12] It is worth pointing out that Banca Etica, MAG6 and La Nef all fund both professional and private loans.

Using ethnographic techniques, I was able to observe the daily work of employees at Banca Etica, MAG6 and La Nef. In particular, I attended weekly staff meetings, as well as meetings between project leaders, borrowers, clients, and meetings involving managers, employees and volunteer members. In the next section, I will carry out a qualitative analysis supported by data such as annual reports, the websites of these organizations, field notes, a few recordings of meetings, and written communication between the actors involved in these organizations, specifically emails and newsletters. In addition, I was able to conduct in-depth interviews with employees and voluntary members of these organizations.

The difficulty of being 'just a little bit' different

Borders between capitalist and civil markets are often porous, and those who act in the latter find themselves exposed to the risks of institutional isomorphism.[13] Of course, one could argue that the model of humanity (and society) created by financial capitalism 'cannot be changed gradually neither by education nor by experience. It can only be abruptly brought into question.'[7] Nevertheless, the assumption underlying this work precisely consists of recognizing that alternative finance would open the possibility of experimenting with an economic model that is different from the capitalist one, even if it acts in the same global market system and needs to respect the same regulations imposed by central banks.[16] The hypothesis to be tested is thus one of a *partially* different finance.

This difference can be conceived as a critique of the present economic system, but a critique which needs to be 'reformist'. This is precisely because MAG6, Banca Etica and La Nef are part of a 'civil market' controlled by the same institutions that govern the financial capitalist market. Moreover, they need to meet clients' financial expectations, which are often not very different from the ones deployed in the capitalist financial sector. For instance, during an interview, a client and voluntary member of Banca Etica related his first contact with the bank as follows:

'The first question I asked when I called them was whether the bank was a real bank. And Employee A, who answered the phone, told me: "Yes, it is". "OK, but… physically, if I come to your office, do I find anyone there?" "Yes, if you come here, you will find me, and Employee B and…" "Then I'll come".'

This concern about Banca Etica's status as a 'real bank' points up the banking needs of the above-quoted client, who notes that he 'needed normal bank services, both from the personal and the professional point of view'. The challenge for Banca Etica, as well as of MAG6 and La Nef, lies thus in the ambition of being 'normal' and 'different' at the same time. Likewise, on La Nef's website it is pointed out that 'from a legal and juridical point of view, there are no differences between La Nef and any other financial institution: its singularity is rather expressed in its philosophy, which is deployed on a daily basis. In fact, La Nef strives to re-establish a relationship of conscience and co-responsibility between two major actors of the financial system: savers and borrowers.'

Banca Etica, MAG6 and La Nef all assess loan applications from both financial and 'ethical' (that is, social/cultural/environmental) points of view. In addition to the financial evaluation undertaken by any bank, they carry out an assessment of the non-economic aspects of the project to be financed as well.[12] Their attitude is nonetheless different from 'greenwashing', implying an instrumental conception of the ethical dimension: the alternative finance sector does not only aim to limit the damage, but rather tries to create positive externalities through its economic operations, by funding projects which have a positive impact on the local area in which they will take place. According to the 'Manifesto for a European Ethical Bank' agreed by La Nef, Banca Etica and the Spanish foundation FIARE, the term 'ethical' (included in the expression 'ethical finance') 'refers to the fact that each human being is regarded as an authority of judgement of value concerning the actions he [sic] does or those actions that are done in his name. Any ethical judgement is by nature individual, although it takes inspiration from a corpus of values collectively acknowledged. No organization can be ethical in itself, but only through the judgement of those who are in charge of its functioning.'[17]

The notion of 'ethical evaluation' can therefore be controversial, because Banca Etica's customers also evaluate the bank according to their own ethical perspectives. For instance, they could judge that 'the prices proposed are not very ethical', compared with other banks from the traditional (capitalist) financial sector, which often offer the most basic banking services for free. The challenge for Banca Etica, and for the organizations working in the alternative finance field in general, is thus to make the saving or borrowing procedures not too costly in terms of financial and time resources, but at the same time to require clients who are willing to accept paying a 'fair price' to participate in this 'alternative economic movement'. In fact, these organizations do not benefit from the high profits coming from speculative operations, and therefore need to price their services from a cost-recovery point of view.

Of course, the concept of 'fair price' is not easy to define, nor to put into practice, but the idea should be that of offering bank services (both for savers and borrowers) at the average price charged within the banking sector. Offering appealing financial products only to attract new clients would be not only difficult from a cost-recovery point of view, but could also backfire. For instance, the above-quoted voluntary member of Banca Etica stated that this institute needs clients 'who believe in the project' and who are also possibly willing to participate in the local groups as active voluntary members, because 'the bank looks for continuity'.

Some of the aspects which make the organizations working in the alternative finance field partially different from the capitalist banks remain nonetheless debatable. For instance, MAG6 has recently decided that it will no longer recompense social capital shares; in general, financial remuneration is low and often it does not exceed the rate of inflation, but the MAG6 assembly has pushed the principle of 'not making money from money' even further by denying any interest to capital shares (which correspond to the only form deposits can take in this financial co-operative). This decision was made in order to allow them to hire a new employee, and also emerged from the idea that MAG6 members will be recompensed with non-monetary goods in terms of both formative opportunities and social gatherings, where participants can establish new relationships with each other or deepen existing ones.

Nevertheless, not all MAG6 employees feel comfortable with this decision, especially in the current context, where inflation is high, particularly for the basic necessities. For instance, during an interview, a MAG6 employee expressed his views as follows: 'Of course, the others [employees] say that we should rather offer another kind of good to MAG members, reducing our dependency on money, but still... Anyway, I think the amount of shareholders will decrease, because most of them did not understand the process we are shaping in MAG, maybe they did not even realize that we have eliminated the return on capital because some people do not even read the *MAGinforma*.[18] But when they realize it... the ones who have [deposited] a lot of money in MAG maybe will take it back...'

The same remark could apply to those borrowers who prefer to seek loans from banks or financial institutions that are able to lend at lower interest rates. In the alternative finance field, the setting of interest rates is primarily based on an organization's profitability and financial stability, because the institutions working in this sector do not derive their income from operations carried out in the field of financial speculation, or 'shadow finance'. They are thus forced to maintain a stable spread between active and passive interest rates to ensure the economic stability of their structure. For example, for Banca Etica – and more so than for other banks – it is essential to maintain active interest (namely, that charged on loans) above a minimum level, because it derives its income precisely from the spread between active and passive interest rates. This policy on interest rates, similarly pursued by MAG6 and La Nef, implies 'great exposure to market fluctuations, making these organizations less competitive in a global context of low interest rates'.[12]

Borrowers can therefore find themselves in the position of not being able to afford 'alternative finance loans' and having to prioritize financial aspects over ethical ones. For instance, during an interview, the MAG6 employee quoted above pointed out that their policy concerning interest rates on loans makes the institution less appealing to potential borrowers:

'If you consider the lower interest rates the other banks charge on loans (obviously, if they do allocate credit)… we turn out to be uninteresting. In fact, some co-operatives […] said to us that we are too expensive… without even being aware of the fact that their users, disadvantaged people, wouldn't get any loan from banks. They wouldn't even be taken into consideration!'

Conclusion

We cannot exclude the possibility that alternative finance will become 'the good conscience of capitalism itself, that which would add morals to its deregulated mind'.[15] However, the aim of this paper was not to show the contradictions and ambiguities of alternative finance, nor to justify its practices against the criticism it receives. On the contrary, I hope to have helped to clarify some of the existing tensions between the elements which differentiate this model from capitalism and the elements which are common to both. In addition, I have sought to highlight the difficulty of putting into place the ideal of ethical and solidarity finance when dealing with the sometimes conflicting immediate demands of the various actors.

Expressing a 'reformist' rather than a 'radical' critique, the alternative finance sector faces the difficulty of meeting customers' financial needs while trying, at the same time, to put in place new banking practices based on different principles. Of course, to help change the dominant economic system, alternative finance needs to mobilize even more actors. In my understanding, this aim could be achieved if these organizations succeed in presenting themselves as a set of different experiences rather than as 'The Alternative'.[16] As Sousa Santos points out, the current critique of the capitalist system could be expressed through 'formative experiments', by which people could be educated in a different way to produce and relate to others.[19] Indeed, any critical thought and practice should help to 'expand the range of possibilities through experimentation and reflection on alternatives capable of representing a more just society'.[20] This can be done 'by going beyond what exists' through the questioning of 'the separation between reality and utopia' and the formulation of alternatives that are 'utopian enough to challenge the *status quo* and concrete enough to avoid being easily rejected as unrealistic'.[21] Regardless of its limitations, its marginality, and its fragility, I conclude that alternative finance proves the possibility of building a *slightly* different kind of finance which would let market economy principles coexist with ethical ones.

Arianna Lovera is a PhD Student studying Sociology at EHESS in Paris and Fondazione Collegio San Carlo in Modena.

1 Mutua Auto Gestione started in Verona but there are now MAGs in Inzago (province of Milan), Turin, Venice and Rome, in addition to MAG6 in Reggio Emilia. **2** Nouvelle Economie Fraternelle. **3** J-L Laville & AD Cattani (eds), *Dictionnaire de l'autre économie*, Gallimard, Paris, 2006. **4** I have already developed this idea in a paper presented to the conference 'Political economy and the outlook for capitalism' (Paris, 5-7 July 2012), organized by the Association Française d'Economie Politique (AFEP), Association for Heterodox Economics (AHE) and the International Initiative for Promoting Political Economy (IIPPE). **5** L Boltanski & E Chiapello, *Le nouvel esprit du capitalisme*, Gallimard, Paris, 1999. **6** K Marx, *Das Kapital*, Berlin, 1867. **7** L Gallino, *Finanzcapitalismo*, Einaudi, Turin, 2011. **8** A Ogien, *Une analyse de l´air du temps*, Éditions de l'EHESS, Paris, 1995; A Ogien & S Laugier, *Pourquoi désobéir en démocratie?*, La Découverte, Paris, 2010. **9** Gallino, op cit ; R Abdelal, *Capital Rules*, Harvard, 2007. **10** M Lazzarato, *La Fabrique de l'homme endetté: essai sur la condition néolibérale*, Éditions Amsterdam, Paris, 2011. **11** K Polanyi, *The Great Transformation*, Beacon Press, Boston, 1944. **12** A Lovera, 'La finance solidaire, travail', *La vie des idées*, nin.tl/14cnDHi **13** L Bruni & S Zamagni, *Economia civile*, il Mulino, Bologna, 2004; L Bruni & S Zamagni, *Dizionario di economia civile*, Città Nuova, Rome, 2009. **14** S Zamagni & V Zamagni, *La cooperazione*, il Mulino, Bologna, 2008. **15** B Frère, *Le nouvel esprit solidaire*, Desclée de Brouwer, Paris, 2009. **16** M Callon, 'What Does it Mean to Say that Economics is Performative?' in D MacKenzie, F Muniesa, L Siu (eds), *Do Economists Make Markets?* Princeton University Press, 2008. **17** Manifesto for a European Ethical Bank (French version), 2012, nin.tl/19xQcof **18** The magazine sent to all MAG6 members informing them about the main activities carried out by the co-operative. **19** B Sousa Santos (ed), *Produzir para viver*, Editora Civiliaçao Brasileira, São Paulo, 2002. **20** EO Wright (ed), *Recasting Egalitarianism*, Verso, London, 1999. **21** EO Wright, op cit; L Boltanski, *De la critique: Précis de sociologie de l'émancipation*, Gallimard, Paris, 2009.

Websites
Banca Etica: bancaetica.it
MAG6: mag6.it
La Nef: lanef.com
Ethical Banking Emilbanca: emilbanca.it
International Association of Investors in the Social Economy: inaise.org
European Federation of Ethical and Alternative Banks: febea.org

Critical perspectives – why a world of co-operatives may not be enough

13
Rebuilding the collective spirit through the experience of co-ops

David Leigh

The economic crisis which became evident with the near collapse of the entire banking system in 2008 had at least one benefit: it prompted a recognition that something needed to be done about the shortcomings of the capitalism which had become the single dominant economic system worldwide following the disintegration of the Soviet Union in the early 1990s.

What was trumpeted by the heralds of free enterprise as the opening of a golden era where markets would rule, where private entrepreneurs would be freed from the shackles of state control and where all would benefit from untold prosperity, was revealed to be an illusion. Almost overnight, the reality of a world marred by extremes of wealth and poverty was brought home to many who had put their faith in a wealth bubble based on soaring property values, personal credit and sovereign debt. Worse still, as the crisis developed, it became clear that there was no easy way to recovery and that millions were being driven further into poverty. Food banks, the modern equivalent of the 1930s soup kitchen, were now on the menu alongside the delicacies served up by TV celebrity chefs. Queues of unemployed workers now contrasted with the queues for those grappling to get their hands on the latest electronic gadget.

With the shortcomings of the system so clearly revealed, even the most partisan supporters of market economies were obliged to consider whether more regulation was needed and whether a touch more social ownership in the form of co-operatives might not be a bad thing. A blossoming of co-ops might give the economy a much-needed boost when capitalists were failing to invest; governments were too broke to do so and reducing budget deficits was their first priority. After all, they could reason, co-ops existed in all the advanced capitalist countries and had existed for many years and there were now one billion co-operators worldwide. Surprisingly, in the United States, the world's most powerful capitalist state, one in four of its citizens were co-operators but the denizens of Wall Street were unperturbed.

Co-operatives, even some which dominated sectors of national economies, exist alongside capitalist enterprises without significantly loosening the grip of capitalism. And therein lies the problem for those who see co-operatives as an alternative to capitalism. Can they be developed to the extent that they transform capitalism into a co-operative commonwealth? The straightforward answer to that question is 'no'. After all, nowhere is there a co-operative which has the capital assets approaching that of even a minor multinational company. Some multinationals have turnovers greater than the GDP of small nations. The idea that co-operatives might challenge and take over multinationals in direct competition is not a serious consideration, the more so because markets are biased in favour of the multinationals who exercise their control both legally by lobbying governments and illegally by corruption and oligopolistic agreements.

There is a second, perhaps less obvious, limitation to the ability of co-operatives to compete with multinationals. It is that co-operatives are best suited to small-scale operations where individual members can directly influence the affairs of the enterprise. Only in small co-ops can decisions be referred directly to the members for approval. If a co-operative expands beyond a few hundred members, then a form of representative democracy has to be introduced to avoid its becoming unmanageable. But it is difficult to see how even this form of indirect democracy could be applied to a multinational co-op, if one were ever to be contemplated. As it is, co-ops are restricted within national boundaries and it would seem that the great virtue of co-ops, their democratic structure, forms a barrier to their development across state borders. They can, and some have, formed trading links with foreign co-operatives but these do not give the individual co-ops the capital required to challenge the largest capitalist enterprises.

Is there therefore a role for co-operatives in transforming capitalism and building a better world? To answer this question we have to consider what capitalism is. It is more than just an agglomeration of capitalist enterprises; it is an entire social system based upon private ownership in industry, transport, finance and almost every other social and economic activity. Its ethos, that of every man for himself and the devil take the hindmost, affects every aspect of government and civil society. It was most openly expressed by Margaret Thatcher in her dictum 'There is no such thing as society' and, while rightwing politicians have subsequently been obliged to dissociate themselves for tactical reasons from this brutal exposition of capitalist values, it is a valid description of the way in which capitalism operates. If today, we in the West live in societies which to a degree care for those who cannot care for themselves, it is not because the essence of capitalism has changed, but because ordinary people have fought for and won, by political and social campaigning, welfare provision.

Today, we can best see capitalism, shorn of its social-welfare veneer, in the way in which capitalist financiers are endeavouring to recover their losses from the 2008 bank collapse by forcing governments to cut almost every aspect of social expenditure, even though premature deaths, disease and malnutrition will increase among the population at large, especially in southern Europe.

The world has changed and is changing at an ever-increasing rate. The application of science and technology has transformed almost every aspect of life and in the advanced countries degrading physical labour and endemic disease have largely been eliminated. Nevertheless, there is a widespread view that things are not changing for the better, a view largely based on the increasing divergence in wealth between rich and poor. For more than three decades a concerted propaganda campaign has drummed home the message that private ownership is good and public ownership is bad. So effective has this campaign been that most leftwing parties in Europe dropped their adherence to public ownership. For them, 'socialism' became a dirty word never to be uttered in public. They went out of their way to assure big business and the rightwing media that they posed no threat to private enterprise. When returned to office, they did not reverse privatizations carried out by earlier administrations but claimed that they could manage capitalism better than the political right. So extreme did this claim to managerial competence become that Gordon Brown could assert that he had put an end to boom and slump, the stupidity of which was exposed by the financial crisis of 2008.

Capitalism can only be changed by a social revolution involving the majority of the people. To do this it is necessary to change social attitudes and restore the standing of public ownership and enterprise in the minds of the populace. How is this to be done and what role can co-operatives play? Not only do co-operatives help poor people raise their living standards but they engender a change in social attitudes. The idea that economic competition is the way to prosperity has held sway for too long. Collaboration in co-ops can and does demonstrate that collective action brings about benefits for all involved, and while co-ops of themselves cannot replace capitalism, they can help to bring about the change in attitudes which is the basis for social change.

If anyone should doubt this, they need only look at the achievements of the 1945 Labour government for proof. The sweeping victory of Labour in 1945 was a surprise to many who thought that the popularity of Churchill, the wartime leader, would win the day for the Conservatives. Buoyed up by an overwhelming parliamentary majority, the Labour government was able to nationalize coal, steel, rail, energy, transport and utilities, and it greatly expanded universal education and social welfare. In new towns around the country it built the 'homes for heroes' which the soldiers returning from the trenches of Great War were promised but never received.

How was all this possible despite a national debt far in excess of that which we have today? If ever the nation was bankrupt, it was Britain in 1945. Vast sums were owed for Lend Lease, under which the US had supplied Britain with food and materials to fight the war but which had to be repaid. Industry and the transport system were rundown, outdated or destroyed by bombing. Almost every commodity was in short supply. What was it in 1945 that enabled the then government to do what our present government is unable to do? Indeed, our present government is destroying what remains of the inheritance of 1945. The answer to this apparent conundrum is really not hard to find. Something fundamental had changed in the attitudes of ordinary people which induced them to desert the Conservatives. It was the war experience of ordinary men and women that brought about the change. Under the leadership of the National Government the nation united in a collective effort to defeat fascism. During the war and afterwards there was a spirit of collectivism, which, for those who never experienced it, is hard to imagine. People were confident that by co-operating they could avoid a return to the deprivation of the 1930s and build a better tomorrow.

Nobody should infer from this that what we need now is a war to give birth again to that feeling among the people that together we can and will make life better for everyone. What we can do is to extend the popularity of co-ops amongst the entire population and help rebuild that collective spirit. The great virtue of co-ops is that they are open to everyone, irrespective of gender, religion, class or nationality and are not, or rather should not be, party political.

In Britain, co-ops are not neutral in terms of party politics. Some co-operative societies sponsor a political party, the Co-operative Party, which has an electoral alliance with the Labour Party. The Co-operative Party was founded in 1917 to win parliamentary representation and secure legislation which would end the discrimination against co-ops practised by the then Conservative and Liberal governments. Failing to achieve sufficient MPs independently, the Co-operative Party entered into an alliance with Labour in 1927. In the circumstances at the time, this alliance was understandable, but even the subsequent election of Labour governments with upwards of 25 Labour/Co-op MPs did not secure for co-operatives the legislation which would put them on an equal footing with private enterprise, a situation which still exists today. The 'New Labour' governments of Blair and Brown, while they had the parliamentary strength, could not find the parliamentary time to enact the necessary legislation, so involved were they with illegal wars and 'modernizing' (some would say, privatizing) welfare, health and education.

The alliance with Labour has had a long-term negative effect on efforts to develop co-ops in the UK. Seen as adjuncts to Labour, co-ops have been regarded by many white-collar workers as organizations for the manual working class alone. Middle-class snobbery, assiduously cultivated during the Thatcher years, meant that large sections of the population became estranged from the co-operative ideal. However, the situation has changed in recent years. Support for co-operative ventures is voiced by all the main political parties now that the failings of capitalism have been brought sharply into focus. The Coalition Government has promised to enact the legislation for so long sought by the co-operative movement.

The Co-operative Party is itself a co-operative but this general trend in favour of co-ops is not reflected in its ranks because membership is barred to anyone who is a member of any political party other than Labour. While claiming to oppose discrimination, it discriminates against any member who is not also a Labour Party member. Those not holding dual Co-op and Labour Party membership are barred from representing the Co-operative Party in local or national elections and their participation in the life of the Party is restricted.

The Co-operative Party has never fully achieved the goals set by its founders and in practice its policies, with minor exceptions, are determined by the Labour Party to the point where it is no longer an independent force in British politics. Most voters are unaware of its existence but the view that co-ops are allied to Labour persists and has deterred many from appreciating that co-operatives have much to offer all sections of the community. The time has come for the co-operative societies to break their formal ties with the Labour Party. The work of the parliamentary group of Labour/Co-op MPs could be undertaken by the All-Party Parliamentary Group for Building Societies and Financial Mutuals with a remit extended to include co-operatives and the funds from the co-operative societies now devoted to maintaining the Co-op Party, some £670,000 ($1,072,000) annually, used to promote the virtues of co-operatives among all sections of the population, irrespective of their voting preferences.

A first step in this process would be to assist Co-ops UK, the umbrella organization for all co-operatives, to transform itself into an active pressure group that would popularize and campaign for the co-operative model to be adopted in all governmental and public-service projects. Every move by national and local government departments to privatize services should be countered by proposals and campaigns to establish co-operatives in those services. The demand should be made that, in any privatization, workers' co-operatives should be allowed to tender. It is not well appreciated by the public at large that co-operatives, along with mutuals, already operate in the telecommunications, energy, housing, retirement, banking, health, education and many more sectors of the economy, and that co-ops are a viable alternative to private enterprise. Co-ops UK, a largely unknown organization, needs to become a leading pressure group as are Greenpeace, Friends of the Earth, the Campaign for Nuclear Disarmament, Liberty and Amnesty International, all of whom get support from all sections of the community.

There never was a more appropriate time than now to place the co-operative alternative before the nation. Britain, the birth nation of the co-operative movement, could become a world leader once again by moderating its market economy with co-ops. By creatively developing co-operative enterprises in all economic sectors, millions would experience the benefits of co-operation. Attitudes to public enterprise would become more favourable and working people would become confident in their joint ability to control enterprises democratically in the interest of the community as a whole. The concept that production and services should be to satisfy need and not greed would develop out of everyday experience and the prospect of transforming capitalism into a genuine Big Society could become a real possibility.

The type of society which the Rochdale Pioneers could only dream of, could become a reality in the foreseeable future – provided the co-operative movement has the courage to rid itself of its old image and rebrand itself as a movement for all the people; a modern movement whose time has come. Co-ops UK has a pivotal role to play in this. The current crisis of capitalism provides the co-operative movement with an opportunity to open up to the wider world. Let it not be missed.

David Leigh is a UK Co-operative Party activist.

14
The false alternative of co-operative choice under capitalism

Chris Tomlinson

One of the current political touchstones is the irresponsibility of the latest capitalist era; the era that produced the banking crisis whose effects we are now living through. Political groups such as UK Uncut have condemned the tax-avoiding antics of the most profitable corporations, while the Occupy movement criticizes the '1 per cent' of bankers and the élite making risky investments with 'our' money. The general public are not free from blame either, it would seem. Eminent economists like Professor Noreena Hertz have berated the indebtedness of the masses, mitigating her chastisement by saying that they were 'living in an era in which it became more shameful not to have the latest pair of Nike sneakers or Gucci handbag than to be in debt'. The government too has constantly resorted to the analogy of the household budget when talking about the national economy. You just *can't* go on spending more than you make and run a family, we are told. Magnanimously, the coalition tells us, our failings as credit-card junkies were reflected in the actions of our erstwhile rulers, borrowing more than they could afford, irresponsibly counting on the good times lasting forever.

In response to the free-for-all of 110-per-cent mortgages, designer clothes on credit, hedge funds and unregulated trading, it seems like we need to return to the Protestant work ethic and its credo *living within your means*. Undoubtedly this means pain in terms of austerity measures, but this is no more than we deserve. While we are rebalancing the books, let's reconnect wealth creation and governance to decent common-sense values. This means making the prehistoric and inefficient elements of state provisions work 'smarter' (with fewer resources) by putting them into the hands of workers and service users.

In this essay I will be arguing that it is in the context of the perceived moral failings of certain operators within capitalism, and the supposed disconnectedness and inefficiency of state and local authority provision, that the case is being made for the co-operative model. I will demonstrate that this debate has been framed in a deliberately disingenuous way to mask the systematic failings of capitalism as a whole and that co-operative principles are no shield against the crises inherent in capitalism which periodically play out, mainly at the expense of the most vulnerable in society.

Furthermore, I hope to show that the co-operative model has been seized by the current government as a way of continuing the Social Enterprise agenda initiated by New Labour in 1997. That is, as a way to marketize areas that were traditionally seen as the realm of state provision, both to reduce state expenditure and to allow private business interests access to new consumers without the accountability or the need to prioritize service above profit that state-managed enterprises traditionally employed.

In demonstrating that, even when they are applied, co-operative principles do not lead to substantive differences between the behaviour of a co-operative and a standard company, we will see that co-operatives in themselves are not capable of overcoming the principal contradiction of capitalism: the class antagonism between the interests of capital and those of the workers.

Although we will see that co-operatives per se, as well as in the way they are currently being used, are not a get-out clause for our increasingly unequal society, I hope to show that they do have liberatory potential. However, this potential could only be fully realized in a society which has already dismantled the structural inequalities of capitalism.

Actually existing co-ops and how they function in society

In discussing the co-operative 'alternative' to capitalism, it seems to be a good idea to start with actually existing co-ops and how they function in society. If we do find a difference between how co-operatives and conventional businesses operate in capitalist markets, we can look to co-operative principles for explanations for these divergences. If we do not find differences, we can try to ascertain if co-operative principles are in fact being applied and, if they are not, whether their application would have a real effect on how co-ops compare to conventional capitalist enterprises.

The kind of co-op that we'll look at first is a supermarket which is a consumer co-operative buying products from suppliers, selling them to members and the general public and employing staff. By starting here we can see the behaviour of a corporate body guided by co-operative principles as it operates in the commodity and labour markets.

The first observation to make is that Co-operative Food, a part of the huge UK Co-operative Group, tends to have prices set at market rates. If we are looking for clear differences between co-operatives and other businesses, the prices of goods on sale to customers (or at least members) is one of the main indicators of difference we would expect to see, especially given that many of the UK's original co-op societies were set up in large part to provide goods at lower prices than other stores. Co-operative stores are clearly trading to make a profit, since without making a profit they would not be sustainable – that much is clear. However, is the pressure on their prices the low cost of equivalent goods from competitors, or has the Group forced down prices across the sector?

It has been argued that co-operative values make markets fairer by their application to influential selling and buying groups. Sonja Novkovic, for example, states 'supply decisions are fundamentally altered in light of co-operative social goals'.[1]

However, this kind of 'fairness' can only be looked at within the strict confines of a competitive market. That is to say, the 'fairness' referred to only means removing market-distorting imperfections. For example in an oligopsony (with many producers and few buyers) Novkovic, following a study by Milford, argues that co-operatives have a 'yardstick' effect, setting the purchasing price higher than the low levels offered in a similar situation without an 'ethically guided' buyer present.

Even by this limited measure, which in reality means nothing more than paying a producer what a lot of competing capitalists agree is the most they're prepared to compromise their profits by, we have a clear recent example of a large co-operative not having the benign effect that is supposed to be inherent. In summer 2012 in the UK there was an extremely stark reminder to misty-eyed co-operative advocates that 'fair' prices are not the inevitable consequence of co-operatives operating in the commodities market. Large-scale national protests were needed to persuade the Co-operative Group (and others) to pay production costs to dairy farmers for their milk. It hardly seems the case, in this instance at least, that the co-operative principle of 'concern for community' goes beyond the typical understanding of 'social corporate responsibility'.[1]

In the same year, the Co-operative Bank was fined £40 million ($64 million) for mis-selling payment protection insurance (PPI) to many of its customers. For a bank which largely advertises itself on its ethical credentials to be caught, along with the rest of the banking sector, duping the public into buying services it didn't need is a clear example of the marked similarities between them and any other bank.

In the United States, meanwhile, the huge agricultural co-operative American Crystal Sugar (ACS) has been behaving like the worst of corporations: locking its workers out after they refused to accept a new contract that stripped them of work benefits, despite huge profits for the company.

While being employed by a Co-op supermarket may be a better prospect than working in Tesco, with a higher holiday allowance and other benefits, the wages are merely 'competitive', which is to say at market value, determined by the least the law will allow and the workers will stand.[2] At the other end of the scale directors receive remuneration which is competitive in another sense – that is to say, paying themselves as much as can be afforded and got away with!

It is simple to find examples of co-operatives treating members, staff and suppliers like any other large corporate body in the market. Of course there are also examples of co-operatives making decisions, particularly purchasing decisions, on ethical rather than simply profit lines. For instance the Co-operative Group is 'no longer engaging with any supplier of produce known to be sourcing from Israeli settlements' – at the cost of contracts worth £350,000 ($560,000).[3] On the other hand, the Group and Co-operative Financial Services are in the fourth year of a contract with Atos, a company infamous for its role in implementing government cuts to disability welfare provision by aggressively recategorizing people with disabilities as fit for work.

To consumers, green and ethical credentials are often seen as desirable attributes in a business, so it becomes difficult to ascribe a qualitative difference to co-operatives' ethical policies over their competitors' statements of corporate responsibility. Even more so when we see a retreat from principled behaviour when it conflicts with profit making, as is the case with the milk-purchasing debacle, PPI mis-selling and the ACS lock-out. While it may seem to be a moot point why a company (or individual) makes a decision if the effect is positive, the distinction is a rather important one. It is often in the business interests of a company to make 'ethical' decisions. If the decisions made are not motivated primarily by a political or ethical stance, however, we cannot expect to see 'ethical' behaviour when the profit incentive is not present.

The Co-operative Group's profits in August 2012 were down a third on their position the year before, so perhaps they do not have the luxury of charging the prices they would like for their goods, or paying what they would like to pay suppliers. Nevertheless, if we see co-operative principles being applied only when economic circumstances will permit it (and without a guarantee that they will be) we must be forced to conclude that there is not a clear distinction between every co-op and its non-co-operative equivalent, at least when it comes to principled (or otherwise) behaviour.

We are faced with the question: if a business buying goods from producers at market costs, paying market-value wages and selling its products at market prices has a different corporate outlook than its competitors, is it really an alternative to them? What are the key ways in which a company can make its social presence felt, assuming it is offering products and services that are available elsewhere? It surely must be in how much its products sell for and in how much it pays to its suppliers and staff. The rest comes under the category of brand identity. Major co-operatives do not display radically democratic tendencies, and meaningful member control does not seem to be a defining feature of them, so I feel we are forced to look at them simply in terms of their economic transactions. A company with principles which it applies sometimes, when it can afford to, is like someone who sports a leaky raincoat only when the weather is fair, yet brags about it come rain or shine.

We have seen some examples of co-operatives embodying the worst practices of capitalist enterprises, and also some of them merely abiding by the logic of capitalism when it comes to accumulation of capital, determining prices and wages. It could be argued that it is uncharitable (perhaps unco-operative) to pick such large organizations as the Co-operative Group's retail businesses, which are, after all, in direct competition with huge adversaries commanding powerful market positions and working with staggering economies of scale when it comes to purchasing. Smaller co-ops are often able to work in niches where they are not directly challenged by other businesses and are therefore able to ignore market imperatives somewhat. Are they therefore able to apply the co-operative principles more thoroughly? I believe we can say confidently that there is not a crucial and substantive difference between a co-operative business and its conventional competitor *per se*. However, let us see what difference, if any, a co-operative which has the manoeuvrability to apply the co-operative principles fully manifests against its profit-mad counterpart.

Is it just a matter of applying the principles?

The current International Co-operative Alliance statement of co-operative principles, which isn't vastly different to those created in 1884, is as follows:

1 Voluntary and Open Membership
2 Democratic Member Control
3 Member Economic Participation
4 Autonomy and Independence
5 Education, Training and Information
6 Co-operation among Co-operatives
7 Concern for Community

It could be argued that the consumer co-operative that failed to pay farmers at least the cost price for their milk was neglecting Principle 7. I am also inclined to believe that if the membership was given a say in what price should have been paid they would have gone higher than the directors were willing to, given the national outcry when the information became public (and assuming that co-op members are at least as concerned about ethical consumerism as the average member of the public, which seems reasonable). This then is also a failure on the second principle.

Given a situation where a region's Co-op supermarkets were run with maximum concern for the community and democratic member control, as we are not faulting them on the other five values, would there be a significant difference between the Co-operative supermarket and that of its rivals?

Let us return to the measures of social interaction of our business, assuming again that the goods and services being offered are available elsewhere. If the membership decides that farmers are really not being paid enough for the work that they do – arduous, risky and unglamorous as it is – they can hike the price paid for milk. If they want to pay their lowest-paid workers more than the minimum wage, they can do so. If they want to cut the prices of their goods to allow customers access to a higher quality of life than they currently enjoy, they can do that too. However, the supermarket cannot enact all measures at once more than to a certain degree. The money has to come from somewhere, and savings are going to have to be made on either the purchasing or the wages side if they want to charge consumers less. Otherwise, customers will have to pay more for products so that producers and workers can be paid more. Another option that the supermarket has is to charge more to customers, pay less to producers and distribute the extra takings as dividend to members, or to directors.

We can begin to see why, in practice, large co-operatives set similar prices to competitors; they are facing the same market conditions and are broadly restricted by the same factors. Even though a co-operative might say that it wants to set its prices lower to benefit customers, many companies would make the same decision to give them a competitive advantage. This means that lower prices for goods (or lower profit made on their retail) isn't necessarily an indicator of a co-operative difference.

Co-operatives (as well as partnerships like John Lewis and

other mutuals) don't tend to pay as high a fee to their board members as do their rivals. In theory, this should give them more room to distribute the benefits of low-priced goods, to pay higher wages and to buy from suppliers at higher prices. However, the £2,118,000 ($3.4 million) the Co-operative Group's CEO received in 2010 can hardly be described as modest, and the relative pay equity in many co-ops speaks more to the unprecedented income inequality in society than to restraint on the part of boards.

Even though it appears clear that the application of the co-op principles is not adequate to cause significantly different behaviour in the large Co-operative Group, there is still the claim to address that larger co-operatives are more susceptible to market imperatives. People who believe that there is a co-operative alternative to capitalism within a capitalist market must believe that co-operatives could replicate any function of a conventional business successfully. Admitting that co-ops competing with certain businesses are incapable of acting as 'co-operatives' would seem to give the lie to this notion. However, for the sake of any 'small is beautiful' advocates, let us turn to a small co-operative operating in a niche.

What about smaller co-operatives?

Birmingham Bike Foundry is very small (it has four members of staff) and it is completely horizontal. It is meaningfully enacting member democratic control (Principle 2) as all its decisions are taken collectively by the members (the workers) and no-one else. It has explicit concern for the community (Principle 7) because its main aims are to make cycling accessible to people in the local area. It extends the concept of community further to encompass minimizing waste and environmental impact by recycling bikes and parts and encouraging sustainable transport. The co-operative is not primarily motivated by profit, and in a sense it is not in direct competition, because it does not have a similar non-cooperative enterprise, forcing it to enter into price wars, or spend money emphasizing its brand difference in values from them.

These then, are three significant ways this co-operative runs differently from any other business and from the large co-operatives we previously looked at: democratic control, genuine community concern and not being primarily driven by profit. Is total adherence to the Rochdale Principles (or at least close enough for the purposes of our argument) sufficient to provide a genuine alternative to capitalism?

The short answer to the question is no. Even though a small co-operative may not appear to be in direct competition, they are always operating in a competitive marketplace. The job and commodity markets under capitalism are totalizing, and the fact that we can imagine we are operating outside of them just goes to show how pervasive their logic is.

For example, the price at which labour is sold is the result of downward pressure by employers, who seek to minimize every outgoing, and the upward pressure of resistance by workers. Essentially, capital (the interests of the employing class) wants to get as much work as possible and pay as little as it can to the workers over the minimum required for their existence.

It is a tautology to say that the prices of commodities are set at a level at which they can be produced for profit by a capitalist because that's what commodities are for. In this case the capitalist wants the price high and the worker (consumer) wants it low. Let us look a bit further into the implications of a labour market and a commodity market where the prices are produced by the tension between labour and capital's power.

A certain large bike chain will pay its workers the minimum wage and import all of its bikes and components in huge quantities from Taiwan. In Taiwan, foreign corporations have been given dispensation to operate in certain 'special economic zones' where the workers labour for (say) 12 hours a day for a pittance and there is little state intervention in terms of taxes. Apart from the lack of labour regulation, there is also complete disregard for the somewhat costly environmental impact stipulations that countries in the West enforce (to varying degrees). The result of this is that products which would be costly to produce in the UK – because of the relatively high labour costs, taxes and environmental regulations – are cheap to make abroad.[4]

As competition for production of commodities is in fact global, there are two main ways of being able to pay UK workers to produce a similar commodity to their contemporaries in the developing world. One is to convince consumers that they are buying a higher-quality product and that they should pay a premium for it. That is to say, selling an equivalent product for more, but asking the public to pay the extra to support British manufacturing, or local produce. The other is to take advantage of the greed of the company selling a product made in Taiwan by selling an equivalent product at the same price, but making a smaller profit on that product. A large corporation making something in Taiwan will be making a very large profit on each commodity because of economies of scale, efficient production and so on. Let us say that the profit margin is 90 per cent. UK workers making an equivalent product could possibly afford to sell it for the same price as the large corporation by making a much smaller profit, or no profit at all after paying the workers. A worker co-op competing with a corporation producing in Taiwan does not have a venture capitalist, board and shareholders taking their rake-off, so it is able to compete by accumulating little or no capital on each commodity produced.

The real fair cost of labour would be the full value generated by their work operating under the socially average conditions of production. That is to say, using the best technology and most efficient production processes developed for the job they are doing. A worker co-op that does not have a boss, directors or shareholders skimming profit off the top is not able to pay its workers the full value of their labour because:

1 They are almost certainly not going to be using technology as efficiently as large capitalist competitors.

2 The prices they charge are restricted by competition (more on this later).

'Small is beautiful' advocates, 'grassroots capitalists',[5] as well as certain strains of co-operators and those on the environmental left, often advocate internalizing the cost of transactions – that is to say, paying the 'full' environmental and social costs of producing certain, or indeed all commodities. The problem with this approach is that even with a radical reduction of superfluous consumerism by an individual, because of the global nature of the commodity market, and the fact that workers are not paid greatly over what they need to live *by design*, most people would not be able to sustain themselves while paying workers in equivalent positions to themselves for their goods and services. Unfortunately, because of the aesthetic religious hang-ups of the green left, the desire for denial and discomfort has wedded itself to a superficial understanding of production in a truly pernicious way.

The 'opt out' notion of anti-capitalism has gone so far as to suggest that the logic of capitalist accumulation can be enlisted to take houses out of the market[6] while it is seen as a given that people can shop their way out of capitalism by buying necessary products made in 'non-exploitative' conditions. While people are still competing with each other to sell their labour to produce mostly useless commodities and services in massive over-abundance, we will not be able to make enterprises serve the needs of humanity. To put it another way, 'no economic system based on private property and competitive social structures can ever be truly virtuous'.[7] This insight comes from one of the early thinkers of the movement: William Thompson. Almost 200 years later, a sentiment which should be commonplace has become largely unthinkable because of the pervasiveness of capitalist logic.

Although the seven co-operative principles could form a good basis for organizing production and distribution, they are not sufficient in themselves to overcome the contradictions of capitalism. This should not come as a surprise to us as we must all know many people who behave in a principled way as individuals, but whose actions also contribute to an unjust social system. In many senses the co-operative under capitalism is in the same predicament as an unwilling wage slave. The bored Human Resources worker knows that she is being sold short when she sells 37.5 hours of her life a week to a pursuit to which she is indifferent. She may have very different personal values than those of the company she works for. She may baulk at the thought of competing with fellow creatures for the finer things in life and even the means to existence, which is in fact what she is doing every day when she shows up to work. Just as the worker is often alienated from their impulses to associate freely with their peers as equals, work on something they feel passionate about pursuing, do something useful for society and take control over their own situation, so too the co-operative body, guided as it often is by people with all the right intentions, finds itself necessarily adrift from its principles, operating in a manner it doesn't identify with, thanks to the imperatives of the situation.

Let us look at another example: that of a food co-operative acting as a buying group where everyone who gets their food through the co-op is a member and shares decision making equally. Let's look at this buying group because its aim isn't at all to make money and everyone is volunteering their time, which should make it even easier to apply co-operative principles.

In the buying group there are 10 members. They get staple goods like rice from a wholesaler and then sell them at cost price to their members. The members of the co-operative are acting in a dual function: they represent themselves as people in need of wholefoods, and they represent the interests of the co-operative in that they ensure there is enough money in the shared bank account to pay the invoice for the food when it is due. It might appear that they are acting in self-interest in making sure that the co-operative is sustainable. But ultimately it is in their interest to get food for as little money as possible so that they don't have to take all the shifts they are offered stacking tins of beans on the night shift. On the other hand, it is in the interest of the co-op to build up a surplus in the bank account just in case someone's payment takes longer than expected to clear one monthly order, or there has been some miscalculation in adding up orders so that one month the signatories need to write a bigger cheque than was expected to the wholesaler. How is this surplus to be generated? By charging members extra on each payment, or by just asking each of them for some money to put in the bank account. In either case the members of the co-operative are being exploited by the co-operative. The fact that, in this case, the exploitation is self-implemented rather than imposed by a board of directors makes it clearer that the exploitation is caused by placing corporate financial interests ahead of those of co-operative members.

Of course, only by acknowledging and making at least some concessions to these corporate financial interests do the members of the buying group manage to keep their operation running. This is still not to say that the interests of the co-operative itself and its members are identical. If, in our buying group, one member falls ill and is unable to work for a week, but their work does not provide sick pay, they will struggle to pay for their staples that month. The other members have the choice of cutting them out of the order that month, or assisting them with paying for it, as individuals, by paying a little extra to make up for the shortfall that their stricken member can't cover. What they don't have the option of doing is simply paying 90 per cent of the order's invoice that month and receiving the full amount, passing the social cost of their member's misfortune onto the wholesaler. The wholesaler would see the illness of a buying group member as irrelevant to the fact that they have supplied a certain amount of goods at an advertised price. If the co-op didn't pay up in time the supplier would be within their legal rights to reclaim the unpaid stock from the co-op, or seek compensation for it.

Regardless of inter-co-op relations, the co-operative itself, insofar as it has external financial dealings, is legally obliged to apply capitalist logic, as enforced by the state, to its transactions. This is even in an ideal case where there is maximum openness of membership, member democratic control and economic participation. All of these democratic features have to be exercised within the constraints imposed by capitalist logic and are tempered by restrictions imposed by the market.

Conclusions

Given that we have seen the application of the Rochdale Principles alone is not sufficient to cause a significant change in behaviour, what is the basis of the perceived difference between the co-operative and its conventional counterpart? Why do many people spend a lot of time advocating, setting up and maintaining co-operatives, and in promoting co-operative values and encouraging others to use them? I see co-operatives as a historical movement to try to implement the ideas of socialism in a practical way, against the prevailing capitalist logic. When co-operatives were first developed, capitalism had not yet asserted itself globally and it was not apparent to workers that it was a system with interests different from their own, which they could resist with collective action. We are now living through a crisis of capitalism and again people are starting to recognize this difference of interests, and the gulf of values between them and capital. This is the reason there has been a bit of a revival of interest in co-operatives of late.

Unfortunately, it seems clear that co-operation on its own is not a challenge to capitalism. The description of the co-operative model that I find most apt clearly demonstrates both their limitations and great potential. It was offered by that famous old anarchist Pyotr Kropotkin, who described co-operatives as: 'experiments which prepare human thought to conceive some of the practical forms in which a communist society might find its expression.'[8]

He demonstrates their limitations by implying that co-operatives are not an exception to, or even a way to organize towards a communist society. But he is generous in that, in a sense, all that is needed to reorganize society along non-capitalist lines is a shift in human thought. Or what Bertolt Brecht described as 'the simple thing/ That's hard, so hard to do'.[9] Kropotkin is crediting co-operatives with this tremendous power.

The condition that Kropotkin sets for the establishment of a communist or socialist society is 'the common possession of the instruments of production'. That is to say, a society in which it is not possible for an employer to make profit out of workers, for homes to be mechanisms for accumulating capital by banks and landlords, and where supermarkets can't pay below production costs for milk.

Would a Kropotkin nowadays imagine that the Co-operative Group is preparing its members to construct radically liberatory structures for organizing the economic base of society? It seems highly unlikely. At best, I believe we can see the Group's ethical policy minimizing some of the worst excesses of labour abuse, while their community dividend schemes probably do more good than corporate responsibility funds' whitewashing.

From the ineffectual to the sinister. The agenda of the current UK government in promoting co-operatives is only too clear. Taking advantage of disillusionment and anger with financial institutions and corporations, the Tories have been talking in the language of empowerment to try and win people over to yet more service cuts and sell-offs. Big Society volunteerism and workfare are twin features of the same vision. 'Everyone pulling together' in reality means the powerless stacking shelves for free to make money for Tesco or Poundland. We can only imagine what the full implications of a government-enforced marketization of what remains of state and local authority service provision for the vulnerable would be. While a group of patients and staff running a hospital with very few resources might be preparation for a catastrophic implementation of communism, perhaps following a bitter and debilitating war, the experience gained would certainly not merit the misery inflicted. If the expansion of the co-operative sector is to be due to the imposition of austerity measures as a method of reducing state expenditure, then the truly principled response should be to not take up the opportunity and to refuse to participate in any further attacks on the lives of working people – even if this means a missed opportunity to expand the co-operative sector. The behaviours and principles that co-operatives are built to embody are not unique to individuals in co-ops, or created by co-operative structures. On the contrary, there are to be found everywhere examples of interactions ignoring the logic of capitalism. While co-operatives are one method of incubating these ideas, we have seen how the expansion of co-operatives can generate a situation where the original values can no longer be applied because of competition, or because the company starts to behave like its competitors regardless of immediate economic imperative.

It is precisely because of the depoliticization of the co-operative movement that there has been no effective ideological challenge to the frankly creepy courting that it has lately enjoyed from the Tory Party. While going along with current thinking and taking opportunities as they arrive might seem to be a way to pull out of the current decline, we have to ask ourselves if the sort of revival we are being offered is not at the cost of the integrity we have left. Would it not be better to build on the differences we have from the capitalist, rather than move into areas where we would be forced to apply the logic of capitalism more rigorously than ever?

There is an alternative to capitalism. That alternative must replace social competition and private property. Co-operatives must surely serve part of the purpose of developing new social and economic structures when that time comes. However, in the situation we are in there can be no opting out or buying out of capitalism. To suggest that co-operatives are an alternative suggests that they can operate simultaneously within and in opposition to capitalism, which is inaccurate. The attractiveness of this falsehood is dangerous, because it can lead us into aiding the degeneration of social conditions out of a kind of co-operative patriotism.

Both the weakness and the strength of the co-operative movement in the UK has been its connection with, and even infatuation with, its historical origins. It is easy to look back wistfully on the 'golden years' of mass membership, political significance and prosperity and not engage with new ideas as a result. However, by viewing the movement as a continuous sequence of events, we can see it as part of a social process, one which has its ups and downs, where the mass of people try to control their own lives. In a deeply divided society where a Cabinet of millionaires defends unaccountable corporate interests and wields the state apparatus, we need the ideas of the co-operative movement more than ever.

Chris Tomlinson is a member of Radical Routes, a network of housing and worker co-ops and social centres whose members are actively working for positive social change. radicalroutes.org.uk

1 Sonja Novkovic, 'Defining the co-operative difference', *The Journal of Socio-Economics* (37), 2008. 2 www.co-operative.jobs/rewards 3 nin.tl/124X9Vs 4 Median hourly wage in the UK in 2011 was around £11/hour. 5 Such as the Adbusters group, which has often claimed to be highly influential in the anti-globalization movement. 6 Roger Hallam, *Anarchist Economics*, 1994. Available on request from Radical Routes federation of co-operatives, radicalroutes.org.uk 7 William Thompson, *An Inquiry into the Principles of the Distribution of Wealth Most Conducive to Human Happiness*, Longman, Hurst Rees, Orme, Brown & Green, London, 1824. 8 Pyotr Kropotkin, *The Conquest of Bread*, GP Putnam & Sons, New York and London, 1906. 9 Bertolt Brecht, *The Mother*, Methuen, London, 1978.

Afterword

What one thing needs to change to make co-operatives the dominant business model?

In addition to the essay competition, for 10 weeks during 2012, *Ethical Consumer* also set up an 'ideas platform', asking visitors to its website to suggest the best answer to the 'what one thing' question above. People were also invited to vote on their favourite ideas, and a 'live voting widget' let them see the effects of their own vote. The website was promoted around UK co-operative networks, including to more than 200,000 ordinary members of Midcounties Co-operative. There were 93 entries before voting was closed and the top 20 most popular entries are reproduced below.

1 We must LEARN how to work in co-operatives. It must be taught

There is security in doing as others do and in doing as we are taught. We are herd animals. The solution must be taught in lower and middle school. Students should have co-ops and participate in them throughout their school years. Then they will have the ability, confidence and desire to be co-operative peers instead of wage slaves or dog-eat-dog professionals.

2 Sustainability and social justice principles should be required of all co-ops

The imperative for environmental sustainability in a world of 7 billion people is an undeniable truth. Businesses of all types are learning that nothing less than systematic and embedded sustainability strategies will do for companies of the future. Co-operatives have a relatively good record in this regard, but until a clear commitment to environmental sustainability becomes unambiguously the eighth co-operative principle (see the website www.ica.coop/coop/principles.html for the first 7), the model itself will not be future proof. And without this clear commitment, winning the hearts and minds of the majority of people on a mainstreaming co-operation project will be impossible.

3 Shoaling – networked co-operation giving the local and small the power of the big

Small and localized co-operatives are more adaptive to the demands of their community but find it hard to compete with the economies of scale of the transnational corporations (TNCs). The result is that ethical co-operatives are widely considered 'value added' luxuries. When large co-operatives (such as The Co-operative Group) successfully compete with TNCs, then there is some loss of ethics and localization.

The solution is holistic. We need to consider not just the increased creation of individual co-operatives but the enabling of efficient and cost-effective trading between them.

We can perceive the problem as the same as insulating our house – but instead of combating heat loss, we need to combat money loss. Potential co-operative trading is currently being leaked to TNCs, and we need to plug the leaks and recycle our money within. This can be achieved by a fully networked movement, offering greater rewards for trading within the network, with disincentives to spend outside. In addition, co-ordinated purchasing can increase economies of scale while keeping each co-operative small, local and thus genuinely democratic. The bridges are the solution, not the islands!

4 We must communicate the value of health over that of growth

'Growth is good' no longer rings true. In a shrinking world we know it's not that simple any more. We still need it of course, but we also need to know it's appropriate – not just another inch on a wooden puppet's nose.

Like a living body, the systems that make our world work need balance, flow and self-regulation to work well. A nervous system in which each cell has a vested interest in a healthy outcome but also plays a part in the decision that might lead to it.

The co-operative model might not be the only way to build and promote healthy business, but it's a uniquely powerful beacon of the very best intent. We're all in this together – let's do something worthwhile.

5 Getting the public to choose co-op before capitalist!

Co-ops with a conscience are at a disadvantage before they open their doors because they will not screw their suppliers to the edge of bankruptcy in the same way that commercial businesses seek profits for their shareholders.

Consumers – that is you, me and all our neighbours, friends and families – need to make the active decision to use their local co-operative even if their products are a penny more expensive because they have paid their suppliers a living wage.

A few of us cannot afford the extra penny but, for most of us, that penny is less than one beer per week, less than one cappuccino or less than one bottle of pop! How many of us cannot afford the price of a drink to make business more fair for all of us!

It is a shame that fair trade only applies to farmers and workers in the developing world! Perhaps the co-op should pioneer 'fair trade at home', so that we know a fair price has been paid for the products that we buy.

6 Promote local co-operatives – people are passionate about local issues

People tend to be passionate about local issues and good causes. We should promote local co-operatives and the fantastic work that they do in the communities in which they are based. Too often it is a well-kept secret!

There are many types of co-operatives out there and local co-operatives coming together at a local level multiply the visibility of co-ops and their effectiveness.

Do people associate capitalism with national and multinational organizations? Is there a danger that a single national or multinational co-op is seen as no different from a national plc?

Big is not always beautiful – *Vive la différence!* Let's promote the fantastic work that local co-operatives do and when they work together they could be a formidable force!

7 Non-profit co-ops

We should remove the idea of profit motivation from the co-op economy in favour of benefiting members and staff in their health, well-being and job satisfaction.

This places the care of individuals and their families above the profit motive. In increasing the social caring attitude there is a possible reduction of the lost working hours through ill-health and a move to a more efficient co-op system.

8 A co-operative government

Instead of a hierarchical party system with leaders, every party should have to be organized like a co-operative. Each paid member would be equally valued, with no prime minister figure.

And every party member who pays to support the party should be allowed a vote or a say in how things are run. That way, the government would have to be sympathetic to co-operatives and that business model. Co-operatives are much more likely to be fair, too.

9 Spread the word

The answer is publicity. The more that people become aware of the benefits of co-operatives, and are sickened by the selfishness of capitalism, the more they will want to join.

We have amazing chances this year. The Co-operative Energy has taken over tens of thousands of consumers from the 'big six' gas and electricity companies. We have to prove that we are better than them. Our tariff is already much simpler, but we must also prove that we are cleaner, greener, sustainable and affordable too. We must push for growth of ALL forms of renewable energy, which will get cheaper. We must advertise everywhere, and spread the word.

10 Social entrepreneurship and co-ops in education

I am a university lecturer. Currently 'employability and entrepreneurship' are a hot potato in education. However, there is little (near to no) emphasis on the importance of knowing there is something called 'social entrepreneurship'. There must be pressures on the government (for schools) and Further/ Higher Education institutions to include co-ops and social entrepreneurship as more than valid expectations for future professional paths after graduation.

11 Make it easier to set up a co-operative

The process that has to be gone through to set up a co-operative is daunting and almost certainly puts many people off. There is also the fear of getting it wrong and being criminalized for doing so. Organizations that help set up co-operatives need to have a higher profile and need to be adequately funded.

12 Co-operative funding for start-ups with citizens' incomes
The main bar to starting any sort of business is the fear that you won't have an income while it is built up. We need co-operative banks and other successful co-operatives to fund start-up co-operatives – with citizens' incomes to avoid people having to stay on benefits and apply for jobs. There would be no interest or repayment. It would rather be done on the 'gift economy' principle that, if and when successful, regular contributions to fund the next up-and-coming co-op would be made.

It then needs advertising so that people know they can take the gamble and still pay the rent. Tables showing who is sponsoring what should be published so that we can all praise (and patronize) those co-ops which benefit the greatest number of new co-ops.

13 Increased support of free-range farming
We spend a lot of our advertising talking about 'the co-operative difference' and make a huge impact on fair-trade farming. However, from the outside at least, we seem to have little interest in supporting free-range farmers.

I understand that there are difficulties with selling free-range foods due to cost. But we could do more to support farmers (financially or with ideas and advertising/branding) and to identify affordable product ideas that would use free-range products, thereby supporting the industry.

14 Local financial co-operatives
A co-operative business society that works for the benefit of its saver and borrower members to invest in local co-operative businesses providing ethically sourced, environmentally friendly and sustainable goods or services for the local community – and that doesn't hold going national or international and floating itself on the stock market as its barometer of success.

To meet needs locally where possible and by starting an alternative to the international corporate distribution chains that we have come to rely on – as with farcical food miles, which are not sustainable in the long term. Such distribution chains could prove to be surprisingly frail if subject to disruption from whatever cause, be it natural or human-made. By meeting needs locally wherever possible, co-operative communities could become more self-reliant, resilient and robust, and less at risk of disruption from events beyond their control.

And an alternative to avaricious, greedy, conglomerating banks, for which the customer is a faceless number to be ruthlessly milked to squeeze every last drop out of them. They gamble their money in the dark arts of investment banking where, if they win, we lose; and if they lose, we bail them out.

15 Networking to evolve a co-op movement

Networking with groups or movements (climate change, transition, fair trade, tax havens, sustainability, etc.) sharing co-op values will raise the profile of co-operative principles and at the same time gather supporters. A resulting co-op movement can function as disseminator of knowledge, encourage support and, in time, reach a critical mass.

16 Less for me and more for us

Capitalism pursues more for the individual. This must be detrimental to the group. Co-operatives teach us to share and only to take an equal share. If there is less in the bank, we all get less. If there is much in the pot, we all get more. The challenge is one co-operative competing against another in the marketplace. The answer must lie in co-operation between co-operatives to share the market. This is a philosophy, not a profit-driven process. As I am sure somebody else has said, we need to require less so that others may have more.

17 Spreading the word about what the co-op movement already does

The British co-op movement already does many things, but insufficient members of the public know about or understand them.

18 No animal-tested products

Wouldn't it be a fantastic and positive attraction for an already ethical company to stock only detergents, hair products etc that have no animal ingredients and have involved no animal testing. This might make the general public aware how many hundreds of thousands of these products are still being tested, when in fact, there is no real need, as has already been shown by the increasing number of Co-op products on your shelves that are backed by BUAV (the British Union for the Abolition of Vivisection).

19 Co-ops need to become multinationals to compete with global businesses

To become mainstream, you need to do what the mainstream does – only better. Globalizing business – whatever its many other faults – does bring economies of scale and often better and lower-cost products. While many larger co-ops do have international supply chains, they remain nationally based. Co-ops may be able to do this by creating 'networks' (or co-ops) of affiliated companies in the same sector around the world – rather than mimicking the more mainstream hierarchical model – but do it they must, or being out-competed on price and quality will be an ongoing issue.

20 Tax incentives for co-operatives

In order to facilitate co-operative businesses, from shops for the public to collections of tradespeople, a tax incentive should be offered. This could engender a co-operative spirit within the workforce[s], keeping them together and, for example, using the tax rebate for common purposes –to provide a uniform/ work clothes/ transport/ tools/ training/ social events and so on.

About the authors: short biographies

Foreword – Ed Mayo

Ed is Secretary General of Co-operatives UK, the national trade body that campaigns for co-operation and works to promote, develop and unite co-operative enterprises. He is a long-term co-operator who has a track record of innovation and impact in his work to bring together economic life and social justice. From 2003 to 2009, he was Chief Executive of the National Consumer Council, merging this with two other bodies to found a new statutory consumer champion, Consumer Focus, in 2008. He was described by *The Independent* as 'the most authoritative voice in the country speaking up for consumers', while *The Guardian* has nominated him as one of the top 100 most influential figures in British social policy. With Agnes Nairn, he co-wrote the book *Consumer Kids*, (Constable, 2009) on marketing to children.

Introduction – Rob Harrison

Rob was one of three founder directors of Ethical Consumer Research Association (ECRA) in 1987. ECRA is a not-for-profit multi-stakeholder co-operative dedicated to the promotion of universal human rights, environmental sustainability and animal welfare. He has worked with:

- NGOs (including Oxfam, Friends of the Earth and Greenpeace) on engaging consumers in their campaigns;
- government departments (including in Austria, Belgium and Brazil) on encouraging the use of ethical consumption and procurement for social and environmental goals;
- consumer organizations (including groups in Spain and Hungary) on researching the corporate social responsibility performance of companies; and
- companies (including the Co-operative Bank, and Lush Cosmetics) on developing world-leading ethical policies and implementing them in practice.

He has edited and contributed to academic work in this area including the 2005 Sage book *The Ethical Consumer* and the 1997 Routledge *Green Building Handbook*. He has been an editor of *Ethical Consumer* magazine since its inception in 1989.

Chapter 1 – Robin Murray

Robin is a Senior Visiting Fellow at the London School of Economics, with a special interest in systemic innovation. For many years he was a Fellow at the Institute of Development Studies at the University of Sussex, working in Africa and Central America. He also had two spells working for radical regional governments in the Global North, the Greater London Council in the 1980s and the Rae government in Ontario in the 1990s. He was co-founder and later chair of Twin Trading, the fair trade company, and was closely involved in the marketing companies that it created jointly with producer co-ops in the Global South to market their products in the North (CaféDirect, Divine Chocolate, Agrofair UK and Liberation Nuts). Robin is a Fellow of the Young Foundation, where he co-authored two books on aspects of social innovation, and an Associate of Co-operatives UK, for whom he wrote the strategic document 'Co-operation in the Age of Google'.

Chapter 2 – Wayne Ellwood

Wayne Ellwood established the North American office of New Internationalist in 1977 and was a co-editor of the magazine until 2010. He was an active member of the NI co-operative wearing a variety of hats including publishing, marketing, circulation management and accounts. During his stint at NI he travelled to Asia, Africa, Latin America and the Caribbean, researching and editing dozens of magazines on a range of topics – from nuclear power to overseas aid to AIDS. But his main interest was (and is) the interplay between social justice, the economy and the environment.

Wayne now lives in Toronto, Canada where he survives as a freelance editor and writer. In the 1980s he worked as an associate producer with the ground-breaking BBC television series *Global Report* and edited the reference book *The A-Z of World Development*.

Later he wrote the first book in the acclaimed No-Nonsense Guide series – his *No-Nonsense Guide to Globalization* has now sold more than 50,000 copies and is a widely used resource in high schools and colleges. He is now writing the *No-Nonsense Guide to Degrowth and Sustainability*.

Chapter 3 – Cliff Mills

Cliff is a practitioner in the law and governance of co-operative, mutual and membership-based organizations. He has written the constitutions of a number of the UK's leading co-operative retail societies including the Co-operative Group, established the constitution and governance of a substantial number of NHS Foundation Trusts, and played a significant part in the development of mutual-society legislation in the UK.

He has worked extensively over the last decade in the development and application of mutual and co-operative models of ownership for public services. These have included healthcare, social housing, leisure services, education and children's services. He has also worked in the voluntary and charitable sector.

The aim has been to create robust models for organizations which are trading for a public or community purpose, with an ownership and governance structure based on user, staff and local community membership.

Recent and current projects include the mutualization of Post Office Limited, Co-operative Councils, library services and community health services. As well as being Principal Associate with the consultancy Mutuo, Cliff is a consultant with Capsticks Solicitors LLP.

Chapter 4 – Dan Gregory

Dan has worked for over a decade to support the development of a more social economy. He previously worked for the Treasury and the Cabinet Office, leading the development of government policy on third-sector access to finance, social investment and the role of the sector in service delivery.

He now works independently under the banner of Common Capital, mainly working to bridge the gap between policy and practice in the funding and financing of mutual and social enterprises.

Dan authored NCVO's report on 'Tax Incentives for Social Investment', the Cabinet Office's Consultation on the Social Investment Bank, HM Treasury's 'Guidance to Funders and Purchasers', a recent report for the Big Lottery on 'Investment Readiness', ResPublica's 'Financing for Growth' and Social Enterprise UK's 'The Right to Run'.

Dan also works to support the development of policy and practice around pop-up and meanwhile use of empty land, shops and property – for example, advising the London Legacy Development Corporation on meanwhile land use post-Olympics, working with Meanwhile Space CIC and 3Space, and helping Merthyr Tydfil Council develop a meanwhile strategy.

He helps run Pop-Up Bristol and Pop Shop Wiltshire and founded the world's first 'pop-up thinktank' – POPse!

Chapter 5 – Daniel Crowe

Dan has been involved in the co-operative movement since being a young member of Woodcraft Folk. He has served on the National Executive Committee of the Co-operative Party and is currently a member of the North London Area Committee of the Co-operative Group.

In his working life he has sought opportunities to promote the co-operative agenda, including researching the potential for mutual housing for the Mayor of London, developing fair trade and community asset transfer policies for the Elected Mayor at North Tyneside Council, and exploring the practicalities of Community Land Trusts at the Young Foundation. With an interest in regeneration, economic development, housing and transport, he has also worked for the Homes and Communities Agency and the thinktank Localis, where he has written a number of reports looking at the changing role of local government. He is now an actor.

Chapter 6 – James Doran

James was born in Manchester in 1985 and he grew up and lives in Darlington, County Durham. His formal education was interrupted by a serious illness and disability. He resumed his studies in 2009 when he began a social sciences degree with the Open University. At the same time, he became involved with labour movement, environmental, and anti-cuts activism, joining the Labour Party and volunteering in electoral campaigns; he also became a member of the Co-operative Party and Friends of the Earth.

In 2011-2 he was involved with Occupy Darlington, an affinity group which held street stalls and public meetings to express solidarity with global anti-capitalist protests and undertake political education on practical alternatives.

James has written other essays about co-operativism that have been published in recent years. 'England's Co-operative Future' will appear in the forthcoming *One Nation* book, and 'Labour's

Co-operative Future' was printed in *The Red Book*, edited by Dr Eoin Clarke and Owain Gardner (Searching Finance, 2011).

Chapter 7 – Nic Wistreich

Nic is a Yorkshire-born, aspiring-filmmaker turned writer (BBC, *The Times*, *Adbusters*), web designer (WAPCEPC, Satyajit Ray Foundation, OccupyUK.info, futuremylove.com), researcher (MTI, Informa) and digital adviser (Scottish Documentary Institute, Cultural Enterprise Office, Film London). He has a passion for the social and cultural potential of networked technology and open source thinking. After running a theatre company with friends, at 19 he co-founded Netribution, a website for indie filmmaking described as 'hugely popular and influential' by *Time Out*. Through this, ShootingPeople.org and three editions of a self-published guide to film funding (fundyourfilm.com) Nic has been driven to find ways to enable independent creatives to work together to get funded and seen in a space dominated by media giants. There's more info at http://visuali.st or twitter/netribution

Chapter 8 – Robbie Smith

Robbie would like to think of himself as a writer and thinker. With 30 years of programming experience, he publishes open source software and is keenly interested in collaborative computing. Robbie gained an MA in Creative Writing for Film and Television in 2000. He has written television, film and radio scripts, all happily waiting to be discovered. He has had a short story published and is currently writing a stage play.

Taking ethics and the environment seriously, Robbie tracks his consumption and each year produces a personal ethical and environmental report from the results. A short film was made last year about his efforts. But perhaps it is his life-struggle that should be regarded as his greatest asset. Robbie is proud to state he has mental-health problems, because he takes pride in his wilful resistance to stigmatization. In 2010, he published a website named Tired Eyes, supported by a mental-health charity, that looked into how the term 'lazy' has been used to oppress and enslave minorities throughout history.

Chapter 9 – Adam Fisher

Adam spent years involved in environmental and anti-globalization campaigns in the 1990s, being found either up a tree or in the middle of a road. In more recent times he has worked in a number of wholefood co-operatives. Over the last three years Adam has been a member of Essential Trading Co-operative while carrying out an MSc in political research at the University of Bristol. Adam discovered that co-operatives are very accommodating when it comes to awkward members constantly changing their hours to fit their academic commitments. Having left Essential in 2012, Adam is now continuing his academic research at Cardiff University, focusing on the early history of the co-operative movement in Britain, in particular looking at regional differences between South Wales and Northeast England in the 1900s. When he's not surfing in Wales, Adam hopes to continue writing articles focusing on environmental politics, and studying the significance of the co-operative movement in relation to the global political economy, past and present.

Chapter 10 – Steve Mandel

After spending more than 20 years as a development economist working both as a civil servant in Africa and a consultant in Africa, South Asia, Pacific and FSU/Eastern Europe, specializing in transport, national and sectoral planning, aid management and budget reform, Steve joined the New Economics Foundation for a while, where he worked on Third World debt, international financial institutions and reform of the international financial architecture. He is now a freelance consultant working on these and other macro-economic issues, a research associate of the Department of International Development at Birmingham

University and a member of the Green Economics Institute.

Steve has always been interested in non-hierarchical organizations. He was (and is still) a founder member of a not-for-profit mutual consultancy working on Third World Development. It isn't technically a co-operative but is so in spirit. He was also involved for a few years in the running of a Steiner school, which has no headteacher and is run by a college of staff.

Chapter 11 – Cheryl Lans

Cheryl Lans did her MSc in Ecological Agriculture and her PhD in Social Sciences at Wageningen University in the Netherlands. Her PhD research was on Ethnoveterinary medicine in Trinidad and Tobago. Cheryl has also taught the History of Food, as well as Science, Gender and Agriculture, at the University of Victoria, Canada.

Cheryl has worked on various projects for the British Columbia Institute for Cooperative Studies (BCICS) and conducted research investigating female leadership in selected co-operatives in British Columbia. Cheryl was funded in 2003 by the Social Science and Humanities Research Council to do postdoctoral research in co-operative studies and alternative agriculture under the supervision of Ian MacPherson. She is the author of a number of books, including: *Movement towards an alternative food economy? Social economy, co-operatives and sustainable agriculture in British Columbia* (2011).

Chapter 12 – Arianna Lovera

Arianna Lovera studied Philosophy (especially Political and Moral Philosophy) in Paris, Turin and Heidelberg. After her Masters Degree in 2008, she worked for a few years in the field of training and education (e-learning in particular) in Turin, Geneva and Holstebro (Denmark) both in the private sector and at the United Nations (UNITAR).

During this time, Arianna kept on reflecting upon the main issues she dealt with in her philosophical studies, namely the contradictions of the capitalist system and the possible emergence of alternatives to it. Sharing the commitment to social and economic justice which gained in strength after the outbreak of the economic crisis, Arianna started a PhD thesis precisely focused on the alternative finance sector as a form of critique of capitalism. In order to meet some human beings from time to time (PhD students' lives can be very lonely), she chose to move from Philosophy to Sociology and is currently enrolled at EHESS in Paris and Fondazione Collegio San Carlo in Modena (Italy).

Chapter 13 – David Leigh

David joined the Young Communist League at the age of 14 and one of his first political actions in 1951 was to canvass for the Stockholm Peace Appeal calling for a ban on all nuclear weapons. He joined the Communist Party of Great Britain (CPGB) at 21 and remained a member until its dissolution. He is now a member of the Co-op Party.

He has a PhD in mining engineering. A career with the National Coal Board (NCB) ended when whistleblowing with two colleagues resulted in a 1973-4 Select Committee enquiry into the NCB's multi-million pound purchasing of mining machinery. Thereafter, he exported engineering equipment.

A former NUM member, he is proud to have been one of Thatcher's 'enemies within'. His political activism includes standing as a CPGB local government candidate, opposing the Vietnam war, campaigning against hospital closures, education cuts, both Iraq wars and for CND and freedom for Palestine.

He fundraises for 'Medical Aid for Palestinians', 'Medical and Scientific Aid for Vietnam, Laos and Cambodia' and 'The Nuclear Education Trust' associated with CND.

He is the author of www.ManifestoForThe21stCentury.info showing how capitalism increases world poverty – a trend which can only be reversed by an economy based on social ownership.

Chapter 14 – Chris Tomlinson

Chris lives and works in two fully mutual co-operatives, Gung Ho and Birmingham Bike Foundry respectively. Both co-ops are members of Radical Routes, a UK federation of fully mutual co-operatives.

At the Bike Foundry Chris and his fellow workers are members of the Industrial Workers of the World union, which seeks the abolition of the wage system and the reorganization of society for the benefit of all. This is something that he advocates and attempts to work towards with political writing and practical solidarity in struggles between workers and capital.

Although we are all forced to live out the contradictions of capital, there are still significant benefits in collaborative and co-operative practice for the individual. Chris produces fiction under the collective identity Yao Ming and makes music in several bands. For him knowledge, learning and the development of a humane and democratic society are an unfinished project by the whole of humanity.

Index

Index

Index

Index

About Ethical Consumer Research Assocation

Ethical Consumer is a not-for-profit, multi-stakeholder co-operative, dedicated to the promotion of universal human rights, environmental sustainability and animal welfare. It was founded in Manchester, UK in 1988.

ECRA produces independent research designed to:
+ encourage sustainable behaviour across the corporate sector through market pressure
+ empower individual consumers to take action on issues of concern to them
+ lead international discussion and research on the potential of ethical purchasing

We produce:
+ Ethical Consumer Magazine - the UK's leading alternative consumer magazine, published 6 times a year. This is available as a paper copy delivered to your door or as a digital download.
+ Ethical Consumer website – which monitors corporate activity daily and contains over 180 interactive product guides, campaign information and forums.
+ Bespoke research - for campaign groups and ethically-minded organisations. Clients include Amnesty International, Christian Aid, the Co-operative Bank and International Consumer Research and Testing.

www.ethicalconsumer.org

About New Internationalist

We are an independent not-for-profit publishing co-operative. We publish a monthly magazine and a range of books covering current affairs, education, world food, fiction, photography and ethical living, as well as customized products, such as calendars and diaries, for the NGO community.

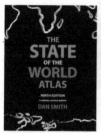   

New Internationalist magazine

The Big Story: *understanding the key global issues*

The Facts: *accessible infographics*

Agenda: *cutting edge reports*

Country Profile: *essential insights and star ratings*

Argument: *heated debate between experts*

Mixed Media: *the best of global culture.*

www.newint.org

Other World Changing titles

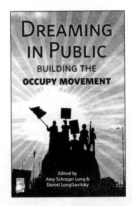

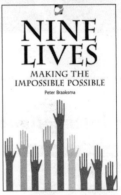

All available in print
and e-book formats.
newint.org/books